Gillian Knox

Key Stage 2
Numeracy Practice Book Year 4

Authors
Peter Patilla & Paul Broadbent

D1331989

Every effort has been made to trace copyright holders and to obtain
their permission for the use of copyright material. The authors and
publishers will gladly receive information enabling them to rectify
any error or omission in subsequent editions.

First published 1998
Reprinted 1998 (twice)
Reprinted 1999
This edition 2000
Reprinted 2001, 2002

Letts Educational Limited
The Chiswick Centre, 414 Chiswick High Road
Chiswick, London W4 5TF
Tel: 020 8996 3333
Fax: 020 8742 8390

Text © Peter Patilla and Paul Broadbent

Design, page layout and production: Moondisks Ltd, Cambridge
Illustrations: Jeffrey Reid, Moondisks
Cover: Ken Vail Graphics

All our rights reserved. No part of this publication may be
reproduced, stored in a retrieval system, or transmitted, in any form
or by any means, electronic, mechanical, photocopying, recording or
otherwise, without prior permission of Letts Educational.

British Library Cataloguing-in-Publication Data
A CIP record for this book is available from the British Library

ISBN 1 84085 058 2

Printed in the UK by Ashford Colour Press

Letts Educational is part of the Granada Learning Group. Granada
Learning is a division Granada plc.

Introduction
to Year 4 Numeracy Practice Book

Numeracy Skills Year 4

This book has been written to develop and improve the numeracy skills of all pupils in Year 4 (ages 8–9).

Each of the nine units of work begins with a double page spread of helpful information. This includes:

- ✓ knowledge needed
- ✓ helpful teaching notes
- ✓ table of what should be learned during the course of the unit

Some pages of activities begin with a Key Skill necessary to complete successfully the activities which follow. Pupils should complete and mark these using the Key Skills answers at the back of the book.

At the end of each unit of work is a summary. This can act both as a quick assessment or as a way to decide which parts of the unit a pupil may omit, or may need to practise further.

Contents

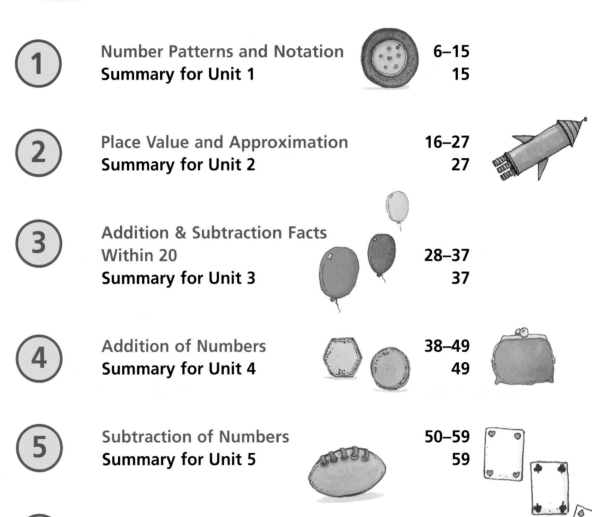

Knowledge needed
✓ recognising odd and even numbers ✓ recognising negative numbe[rs]
✓ telling the time ✓ simple measurement notatio[n]

Helpful facts

Recognising odd and even numbers

All even numbers end in:

0, 2, 4, 6 or 8

examples

40, 52, 94, 136, 378

All odd numbers end in:

1, 3, 5, 7 or 9

examples

31, 63, 75, 237, 469

Multiples

The multiples of 3 are:

3, 6, 9, 12, 15, ...

The multiples of 4 are:

4, 12, 16, 20, 24, ...

Multiples of 2 are always even:

2, 14, 16, 28, 30, 62, ...

Multiples of 5 always end in 5 or 0:

5, 10, 15, 20, 25, 30, ...

Multiples of 10 always end in 0:

10, 20, 30, 40, 50, 60, ...

Factors

Factors are numbers which will divide exactly into other numbers.

The factors of 12 are:

1, 2, 3, 4, 6 and 12

The factors of 15 are:

1, 3, 5 and 15

5 is a factor of:

5, 10, 15, 20, ...

7 is a factor of:

7, 14, 21, 28, ...

Postive & negative numbers

negative numbers   positive numbers

...–6, –5, –4, –3, –2, –1, 0, 1, 2, 3, 4, 5, 6...

Prime numbers

Prime numbers are numbers which can only be divided by themselves and 1, e.g.

2, 3, 5, 7, 11, 13, 17, 19

Square numbers

To make a square number, multiply a number by itself:

$3 \times 3 = 9$

9 is a square number

$7 \times 7 = 49$

49 is a square number

Measures

mm = millimetres   g = grams

m*l* = millilitres   cm = centimetres

kg = kilogram   *l* = litres m = metres

10 mm = 1 cm   100 cm = 1 m

1000 mm = 1 metre   1000 g = 1 kg

1000 ml = 1 litre

analogue time

o'clock

55 mins past

50 mins past

45 mins past

40 mins past

35 mins past

30 mins past

5 mins past

10 mins past

15 mins past

20 mins past

25 mins past

seven fifteen or 15 minutes past 7
- The small hand shows the hour
- The longer hand shows how many minutes past the hour

digital time

shows the hour

4:30

shows how many minutes past

four thirty or 30 minutes past 4

Learning outcomes for UNIT 1

✓ recognises negative numbers in context
✓ recognises and extends counting patterns
✓ recognises odd and even numbers of any size
✓ recognises multiples of 2, 3, 4, 5, 10 and 100
✓ recognises squares of numbers up to 10 x 10
✓ recognises simple multiples and factors
✓ recognises time using digital and analogue clocks
✓ knows simple measurement notation and equivalences

Sequences

A ....

Copy and write the next two numbers in each pattern.

1. 7, 9, 11, 13, ⊘, ⊘

2. 23, 25, 27, 29, ⊘, ⊘

3. 115, 117, 119, 121, ⊘, ⊘

4. 461, 463, 465, 467, ⊘, ⊘

5. 230, 250, 270, 290, ⊘, ⊘

6. 75, 70, 65, 60, ⊘, ⊘

7. 800, 700, 600, 500, ⊘, ⊘

8. 45, 42, 39, 36, ⊘, ⊘

9. 200, 190, 180, 170, ⊘, ⊘

10. 60, 56, 52, 48, ⊘, ⊘

B ....

Copy and write the missing four numbers in each pattern.

1. △, △, 13, 18, 23, 28, △, △

2. △, △, 33, 43, 53, 63, △, △

3. △, △, 16, 19, 22, 25, △, △

4. △, △, 10, 14, 18, 22, △, △

5. △, △, 28, 37, 46, 55, △, △

6. △, △, 25, 22, 19, 16, △, △

7. △, △, 72, 62, 52, 42, △, △

8. △, △, 54, 49, 44, 39, △, △

9. △, △, 62, 58, 54, 50, △, △

10. △, △, 73, 64, 55, 46, △, △

C ....

Copy and write the missing two numbers in each pattern.

1. 3, 2, 1, 0, ⊖, ⊖

2. 6, 4, 2, 0, ⊖, ⊖

3. 15, 10, 5, 0, ⊖, ⊖

4. 30, 20, 10, 0, ⊖, ⊖

5. 12, 8, 4, 0, ⊖, ⊖

6. ⊖, ⊖, -2, -1, 0, 1

7. ⊖, ⊖, -2, 0, 2, 4

8. ⊖, ⊖, -2, 3, 8, 13

9. ⊖, ⊖, -2, 2, 6, 10

10. ⊖, ⊖, -2, 1, 4, 7

D ....

Copy and write the missing two numbers in each pattern.

1. 14, 16, ..., ..., 22, 24

2. 32, ..., 40, 44, ..., 52

3. 35, ..., 45, 50, 55, ...

4. ..., 30, ..., 36, 39, 42

5. ..., 70, 80, ..., 100, 110

6. 36, ..., 30, 27, 24, ...

7. 70, 65, ..., ..., 50, 45

8. 130, 120, 110, ..., 90, ...

9. ..., 44, ..., 36, 32, 28

10. ..., 70, 68, ..., 64, 62

Special Numbers

A

Write the square of these numbers.

1. 4   3. 2   5. 6   7. 8   9. 10
2. 1   4. 3   6. 5   8. 7   10. 9

B

Write which numbers have been squared to make these.

1. 4   3. 1   5. 64   7. 25   9. 4
2. 16   4. 9   6. 81   8. 100   10. 49

C

Write the odd factors of: Write the even factors of:

1. twelve   3. twenty   5. six   7. twelve
2. eighteen   4. twenty-four   6. ten   8. fourteen

D

Write the mystery numbers.

1. I am the next multiple of 4 after 32.
2. I am the multiple of 3 before 27.
3. I am the next even multiple of 5 after 50.
4. I am the next odd multiple of 3 after 21.
5. I am the even multiple of 3 before 42.
6. I am the odd multiple of 5 before 65.
7. I am the multiple of 4 which is square.
8. I am the multiple of 10 which is square.

E

Write the odd one out in each set. Write why each number is the odd one out.

1. 5 65 24 40 60   4. 32 36 34 38 35   7. 36 39 30 35 33
2. 1 4 36 35 81   5. 300 500 600 400 550   8. 50 90 60 85 80
3. 41 43 46 45 47   6. 40 24 45 36 44   9. 3 7 25 40 39

Negative Numbers

A

Write the finishing numbers.

−10　　　　　−5　　　　　　0　　　　　5　　　　　　10

1.　−9 ⁺⁴→ ▭　　　6.　−5 ⁺²→ ▭　　　11.　−9 ⁺¹⁰→ ▭

2.　−4 ⁺³→ ▭　　　7.　−10 ⁺⁸→ ▭　　　12.　−7 ⁺¹²→ ▭

3.　−8 ⁺²→ ▭　　　8.　−7 ⁺⁷→ ▭　　　13.　−10 ⁺¹³→ ▭

4.　−2 ⁺¹→ ▭　　　9.　−6 ⁺⁵→ ▭　　　14.　−8 ⁺¹⁴→ ▭

5.　−8 ⁺⁶→ ▭　　　10.　−4 ⁺²→ ▭　　　15.　−5 ⁺⁵→ ▭

B

Write the finishing numbers.

−10　　　　　−5　　　　　　0　　　　　5　　　　　　10

1.　$10 \xrightarrow{-9}$　　6.　$7 \xrightarrow{-2}$　　11.　$0 \xrightarrow{-4}$

2.　$6 \xrightarrow{-8}$　　7.　$5 \xrightarrow{-1}$　　12.　$5 \xrightarrow{-10}$

3.　$3 \xrightarrow{-3}$　　8.　$2 \xrightarrow{-0}$　　13.　$4 \xrightarrow{-8}$

4.　$9 \xrightarrow{-6}$　　9.　$1 \xrightarrow{-1}$　　14.　$2 \xrightarrow{-6}$

5.　$8 \xrightarrow{-7}$　　10.　$4 \xrightarrow{-3}$　　15.　$8 \xrightarrow{-9}$

Negative Numbers

C

Use a number line to write the differences between these numbers.

1. (−1) (−5)   5. (−7) (−3)   9. (−1) (−7)   13. (−6) (−5)   17. (0) (−5)

2. (−6) (−10)   6. (−2) (−8)   10. (−3) (−10)   14. (−1) (−9)   18. (−7) (8)

3. (−4) (−3)   7. (−5) (−10)   11. (−6) (−4)   15. (−5) (5)   19. (−9) (6)

4. (−9) (−2)   8. (−2) (−6)   12. (8) (−10)   16. (5) (−10)   20. (8) (−5)

D

Write the temperature shown on each thermometer.

1.   2.   3.   4.   5.

1.4

Measures Notation and Equivalences

A ....

Copy and complete these equivalences.

1. ☐ cm = 1 metre
2. ☐ mm = 1 metre
3. ☐ mm = 1 cm

4. ☐ g = 1 kilogram
5. ☐ ml = 1 litre
6. $\frac{1}{2}$ metre = ☐ cm

7. $\frac{1}{2}$ kilogram = ☐ g
8. $\frac{1}{2}$ litre = ☐ ml
9. $\frac{1}{2}$ cm = ☐ mm

B ....

Write < > or = between the amounts.

1. 5 mm ☐ 1 cm
2. 5 cm ☐ 1 metre
3. 5 metre ☐ 1 cm
4. 5 cm ☐ 1 mm

5. 5 mm ☐ 1 metre
6. 10 mm ☐ 1 cm
7. 10 cm ☐ 1 metre
8. 10 metres ☐ 1 cm

9. 10 cm ☐ 1 mm
10. 10 mm ☐ 1 metre
11. 100 cm ☐ 1 metre
12. 100 mm ☐ 1 cm

C .... **D** ....

Write the length to which each arrow points.

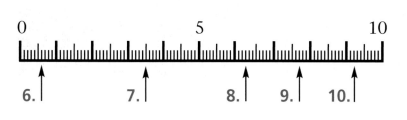

0   5   10

1.↑   2.↑   3.↑   4.↑   5.↑

0   5   10

6.↑   7.↑   8.↑ 9.↑ 10.↑

Write in ml how much is in each container.

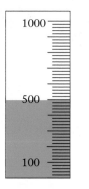

Reading the Time

A

Write the times shown on these clocks.

B

Write the times shown on these clocks.

Reading the Time

C

Write these times one hour later.

1. 4:30	**2.** 8:15	**3.** 12:30	**4.** 1:45
5. 6:25	**6.** 10:05	**7.** 5:50	**8.** 7:40
9. 2:05	**10.** 5:00	**11.** 3:45	**12.** 9:30

D

Write these times one hour earlier.

1. 1:45	**2.** 10:15	**3.** 7:45	**4.** 2:30
5. 4:25	**6.** 9:40	**7.** 3:05	**8.** 12:35

E

Write these afternoon times in order.

1.	5 minutes past 4	2.30	half past 3	noon
2.	6.15	eight thirty	4.05	half past 4
3.	15 minutes past 3	half past 3	3.45	3.20

14

Summary for Unit 1

A

Write the missing numbers.

1. 1, 4, 9, 16, 25, ..., ...
2. 67, 65, 63, 61, 59, ..., ...
3. 30, 27, 24, 21, 18, ..., ...
4. 7, 11, 15, 19, 23, ..., ...

B

1. Write the square of 7.
2. Write which number has been squared to make 81.
3. Write an odd factor of 12.
4. Write the next multiple of 3 after 15.
5. Write the next even multiple of 5 after 20.

C

Write the temperature change between the two thermometers.

D

Write the time.   Write 1 hour later.   Write 1 hour earlier.

8:30   6:30

E

Copy and complete.

1. ☐ cm = 1 m   2. ☐ mm = 1 cm   3. ☐ ml = 1 litre   4. ☐ g = 1 kg

Copy and write < > or = between the numbers.

5. 10 mm ☐ 1 cm   6. 10 cm ☐ 1 m   7. 100 mm ☐ 1 cm

Helpful facts

Place Value and Approximation

Digits
There are ten digits:
0, 1, 2, 3, 4, 5, 6, 7, 8, 9

3-digit numbers
These are all the whole
numbers from 100 to 999:

hundreds   tens   units

2 3 5
200 + 30 + 5

Spike abacus

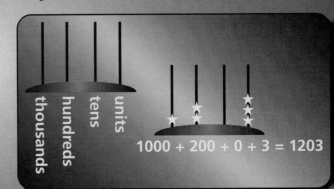

1000 + 200 + 0 + 3 = 1203

Thousands

hundred thousands	ten thousands	thousands	hundreds	tens	units

A shorthand way to write a thousand is to use k:

3000 = 3k   50,000 = 50k

Commas are sometimes used to separate thousands from hundreds.

Rounding

To the nearest 10:
look at the last digit, if less than 5
round down, otherwise round up

examples

81 round down 80
404 round down 400
15 round up 20
798 round up 800

To the nearest 100:
look at last two digits, if less than 50
round down, otherwise round up

332 round down 300
640 round down 600
850 round up 900
283 round up 300

To the nearest 1000:
look at the last three digits, if less than
500 round down, otherwise round up

4390 round down 4000
6702 round up 7000
8500 round up 9000

To the nearest pound:
look at the pennies, if less than 50p
round down, otherwise round up

£4.49 round down £4
£6.18 round down £6
£7.50 round up £8
£4.74 round up £5

Learning outcomes for UNIT 2

✓ reads and writes numbers to at least 10,000
✓ knows the value of digits in 5-digit numbers
✓ knows 1, 10, 100, 1000 more than whole numbers
✓ knows 1, 10, 100, 1000 less than whole numbers
✓ estimates approximate and round numbers & measurements
  to nearest 10, 100 & 1000
✓ multiplies and divides whole numbers by 10 and 100
✓ uses place value in money and measures
✓ understands vocabulary of number

2.1

Place Value for TH H TU

Key Skills ✔

Write the value of the underlined digit.

1. 6<u>4</u>5
2. 36<u>4</u>
3. <u>7</u>05
4. 7<u>9</u>9

Check your answers.

Write these using numbers.

5. Three hundred and two.
6. Six hundred and fifty.
7. Ninety-six.
8. Seven hundred and fifteen.

A

Write the value of the underlined digit.

1. <u>4</u>000
2. 16<u>2</u>4
3. 3<u>8</u>27
4. <u>3</u>522
5. 6<u>5</u>55
6. <u>8</u>086
7. 63<u>1</u>4
8. <u>8</u>787
9. 63<u>4</u>0
10. <u>9</u>324
11. 640<u>5</u>
12. 66<u>0</u>7
13. 724<u>0</u>
14. 3<u>6</u>21
15. 74<u>1</u>4

B

Break each number up into thousands, hundreds, tens and units,
e.g. 2000 + 500 + 20 + 3 = 2523

1. 6421
2. 1250
3. 4027
4. 3202
5. 5165
6. 4500
7. 3784
8. 1699
9. 4422
10. 8175
11. 4678
12. 7251
13. 5007
14. 2136
15. 8592

C

Write the number shown on each abacus.

1.  2. 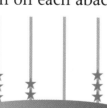 3. 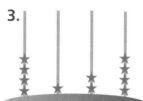 4.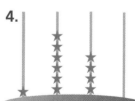

D

Arrange each set of digits to make the largest and smallest numbers.

1. | 4 | 3 |
   | 1 | 7 |

2. | 5 | 0 |
   | 6 | 2 |

3. | 9 | 1 |
   | 2 | 4 |

4. | 6 | 4 |
   | 0 | 7 |

5. | 8 | 7 |
   | 1 | 4 |

6. | 7 | 4 |
   | 3 | 8 |

Place Value for Thousands

Write the number shown on each abacus.

1. 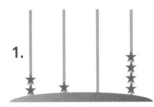 **2.** 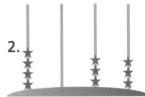 **3.**

Write the value of the digit in the square.
Check your answers.

4. 4 │7│ 6 5   **5.** │3│ 8 0 4   **6.** 7 2 │2│ 4

A

Write the number shown on each abacus.

1.  **2.** 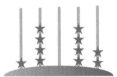 **3.**  **4.**

5.  **6.** 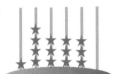 **7.**  **8.**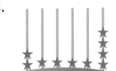

Can you say the numbers in words?

B

Write these as numbers using digits.

1. Twenty-four thousand.
2. Seventy thousand.
3. Ten thousand.
4. Eighty-one thousand.
5. Ninety-nine thousand.

6. Sixteen thousand two hundred.
7. Twelve thousand eight hundred.
8. Twenty thousand and forty.
9. Sixty thousand and eighty.
10. Forty thousand and two.

Place Value for Thousands

C

Write these numbers in words.

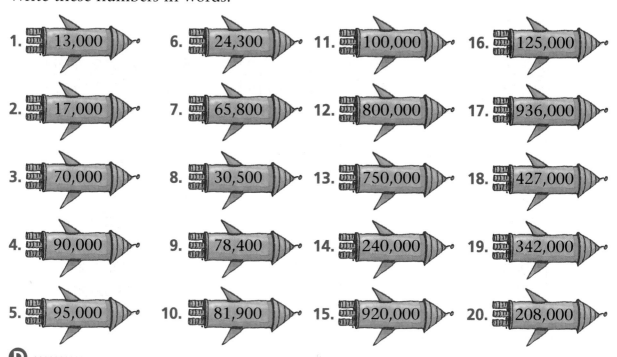

1. 13,000
2. 17,000
3. 70,000
4. 90,000
5. 95,000

6. 24,300
7. 65,800
8. 30,500
9. 78,400
10. 81,900

11. 100,000
12. 800,000
13. 750,000
14. 240,000
15. 920,000

16. 125,000
17. 936,000
18. 427,000
19. 342,000
20. 208,000

D

Remember k is shorthand for 1000.
Write these in full.

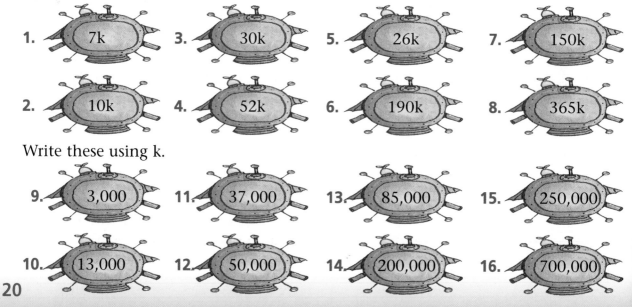

1. 7k
2. 10k
3. 30k
4. 52k
5. 26k
6. 190k
7. 150k
8. 365k

Write these using k.

9. 3,000
10. 13,000
11. 37,000
12. 50,000
13. 85,000
14. 200,000
15. 250,000
16. 700,000

20

Using Place Value

A

The dials show kilometres.
Write each reading after one more kilometre.

1. | 0 | 0 | 1 | 2 | 4 | 9 |
2. | 0 | 0 | 3 | 0 | 6 | 9 |
3. | 0 | 0 | 2 | 6 | 8 | 9 |

4. | 0 | 0 | 7 | 1 | 9 | 9 |
5. | 0 | 0 | 3 | 4 | 9 | 9 |
6. | 0 | 0 | 1 | 0 | 9 | 9 |

7. | 0 | 0 | 4 | 9 | 9 | 9 |
8. | 0 | 0 | 6 | 9 | 9 | 9 |
9. | 0 | 0 | 3 | 7 | 9 | 9 |

B

Write which numbers went into the machine.   → In | +1 | Out →

1.
IN	OUT
	3000
	5000
	6000
	8000

2.
IN	OUT
	10,000
	40,000
	60,000
	90,000

3.
IN	OUT
	100,000
	300,000
	700,000
	900,000

C

Add 10 to each number.

1. 4360
2. 7250
3. 9960
4. 4910
5. 6490
6. 13,510
7. 27,200
8. 56,490
9. 30,400
10. 36,690
11. 1889
12. 1898
13. 1998
14. 1999
15. 1888

D

Increase each number by 100.

1. 6320
2. 2550
3. 7300
4. 8255
5. 9420
6. 24,900
7. 35,950
8. 64,975
9. 28,925
10. 42,325

Increase each number by 1000.

11. 16,000
12. 28,000
13. 35,000
14. 46,000
15. 74,000
16. 36,450
17. 29,000
18. 89,000
19. 99,000
20. 129,000

Estimation of Numbers

A

Estimate which decade number each arrow points to.

0　　　　　　　1.　　　　　　　2.　　　　　　　3.　　　　　100

0　　4.　　　　　　　5.　100　　　　　　　　6.　　　　200

B

Estimate which decade number each arrow points to.

0　　　　　　　1.　　　　　　　2.　　　　　　　3.　　　　1000

0　　4.　　　　　　　5.　500　　　　　　　　6.　　　　1000

C

Estimate which hundred number each arrow points to.

0　　　　　　　1.　　　　　　　2.　　　　　　　3.　　　　1000

0　　　　　　4.　　　　1000　　5.　6.　　　　　　2000

D

Estimate which hundred number each arrow points to.

0　　　　　　　1.　　　　　　　2.　　　　　　　3.　　　　6000

0　　　　　　4.　　　　　　　5.　6.　　　　　10,000

22

Approximation of Numbers

A

Round each number to the nearest 10.

1. 63	**4.** 65	**7.** 517	**10.** 294	**13.** 1248
2. 48	**5.** 341	**8.** 652	**11.** 697	**14.** 3655
3. 74	**6.** 629	**9.** 395	**12.** 792	**15.** 6799

B

Round each number to the nearest 10.

1. 874	**4.** 360	**7.** 1799	**10.** 7962	**13.** 47,963
2. 452	**5.** 4542	**8.** 3389	**11.** 3976	**14.** 34,949
3. 649	**6.** 2625	**9.** 5935	**12.** 4951	**15.** 16,917

C

Round each number to the nearest pound.

1. £1.46	**4.** £4.50	**7.** £17.65	**10.** £34.14	**13.** £123.37
2. £7.38	**5.** £13.65	**8.** £19.75	**11.** £69.50	**14.** £199.59
3. £9.58	**6.** £17.28	**9.** £29.97	**12.** £45.46	**15.** £230.90

D

Round each number to the nearest 1000.

1. 3400	**4.** 5500	**7.** 5100	**10.** 7650	**13.** 3950
2. 2300	**5.** 6700	**8.** 4200	**11.** 2250	**14.** 8350
3. 1800	**6.** 7900	**9.** 6750	**12.** 4550	**15.** 9450

E

Write each amount to the nearest 1000.

1. 13,200	**4.** 16,800	**7.** 19,600	**10.** 69,250	**13.** 49,125
2. 18,500	**5.** 25,100	**8.** 39,900	**11.** 59,850	**14.** 69,625
3. 12,700	**6.** 40,400	**9.** 39,650	**12.** 79,550	**15.** 99,725

Measurement Numbers

A

Write the length of each rod to the nearest centimetre.

1.

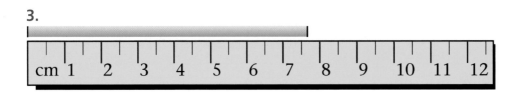

2.

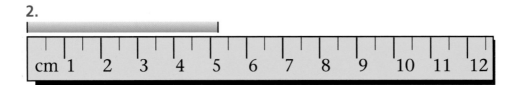

3.

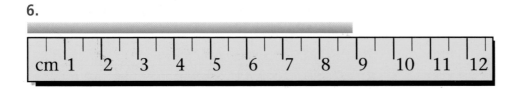

4.

5.

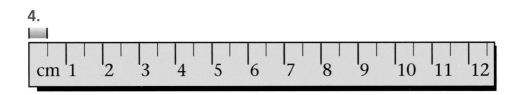

6.

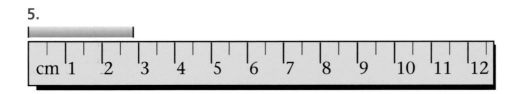

Measurement Numbers

B ....

Write each weight to the nearest kilogram.

1. 4 kg 350 g	**7.** 6 kg 950 g	**13.** 1250 g	**19.** 9450 g
2. 2 kg 500 g	**8.** 3 kg 400 g	**14.** 4640 g	**20.** 6350 g
3. 7 kg 750 g	**9.** 5 kg 850 g	**15.** 5500 g	**21.** 3120 g
4. 3 kg 250 g	**10.** 7 kg 450 g	**16.** 6300 g	**22.** 8740 g
5. 4 kg 800 g	**11.** 2430 g	**17.** 7390 g	**23.** 1870 g
6. 2 kg 100 g	**12.** 3750 g	**18.** 4560 g	**24.** 9000 g

C ....

Measure the length of each line to the nearest centimetre.

1.
2.
3.
4.
5.
6.
7.
8.

D ....

Write each capacity to the nearest litre.

1. 2 *l* 400 m*l*	**7.** 6 *l* 500 m*l*	**13.** 3600 m*l*	**19.** 4250 m*l*
2. 5 *l* 600 m*l*	**8.** 5 *l* 800 m*l*	**14.** 1300 m*l*	**20.** 2550 m*l*
3. 3 *l* 300 m*l*	**9.** 8 *l* 200 m*l*	**15.** 6800 m*l*	**21.** 3200 m*l*
4. 2 *l* 900 m*l*	**10.** 7 *l* 500 m*l*	**16.** 3450 m*l*	**22.** 9680 m*l*
5. 1 *l* 700 m*l*	**11.** 2500 m*l*	**17.** 4750 m*l*	**23.** 10,170 m*l*
6. 4 *l* 100 m*l*	**12.** 5400 m*l*	**18.** 5650 m*l*	**24.** 6010 m*l*

2.7

Place Value and Powers of 10

A ....

Multiply each number by 10.

1. 36 **3.** 77 **5.** 83 **7.** 24 **9.** 30 **11.** 120 **13.** 246 **15.** 577

2. 69 **4.** 45 **6.** 51 **8.** 88 **10.** 92 **12.** 152 **14.** 363 **16.** 861

B ....

Divide each number by 10.

1. 380	**6.** 940	**11.** 2500	**16.** 6100
2. 400	**7.** 230	**12.** 7000	**17.** 9800
3. 550	**8.** 390	**13.** 4600	**18.** 1200
4. 420	**9.** 600	**14.** 5200	**19.** 6700
5. 670	**10.** 860	**15.** 9500	**20.** 3800

C ....

Look at the function machine. Copy and complete each table.

1.
→ In | ÷10 | Out →

In	300		800		6000		3500	
Out		60		75		800		950

2.
→ In | ×10 | Out →

In	40		65		500		550	
Out		700		350		3000		9500

D ....

Multiply each number by 100.

1. 13	**6.** 45	**11.** 80	**16.** 700
2. 19	**7.** 84	**12.** 20	**17.** 450
3. 16	**8.** 92	**13.** 200	**18.** 750
4. 15	**9.** 50	**14.** 300	**19.** 850
5. 36	**10.** 70	**15.** 800	**20.** 350

Summary for Unit 2

1. What does the 9 represent in 4930?
2. How many thousands are in 3245?
3. Write six thousand four hundred using digits.
4. Write the number shown on the abacus.

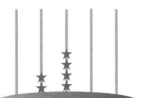

B

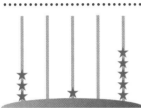

1. Write the number shown on the abacus.
2. Write 85,000 using words.
3. Write twelve thousand five hundred using digits.
4. Write 25k in full, using digits.

C

1. Write the whole number which follows 2999.
2. Add 10 to 3990.
3. Add 100 to 9950.
4. Increase 69,000 by 1000.

D

1. Estimate which number the arrow points to.

0   100

2. Round 4600 to the nearest thousand.
3. Round £15.45 to the nearest pound.
4. Round 3500 g to the nearest kg.

E

Write the missing number.

1. 56 → In | ×10 | Out → ☐

2. ☐ → In | ×10 | Out → 3600

3. 8000 → In | ÷10 | Out → ☐

4. 30 → In | ×100 | Out → ☐

27

Knowledge needed
✓ recall of addition facts to 20
✓ recall of subtraction facts within 20
✓ language of addition and subtraction facts

Helpful facts

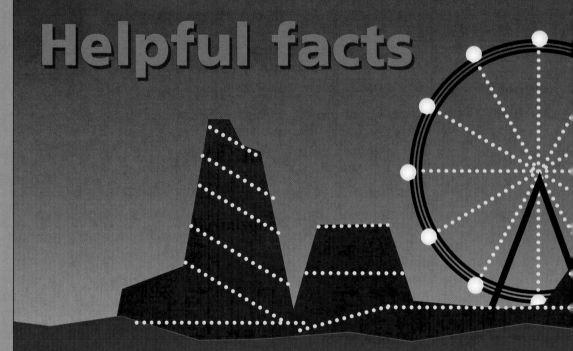

Any way round
The order of adding two
numbers does not matter:
2 + 15 = 15 + 2
7 + 8 = 8 + 7

Pairs which total 10
The number pairs which total
10 are very important:
10,0 9,1 8,2 7,3 6,4 5,5

Brackets
Always work out the sum in
brackets first:
15 – (10 – 3)

work out first
then   15 – 7 = 8

Quick methods
Add on 9:
add 10 then –1   26 + 9 = 35
Subtract 9
–10 then add 1   45 – 9 = 36

Difference
To find the number difference
between two numbers, subtract
them. The difference between
8 13 is
13 – 8 = 5
The difference is 5.

Extending subtraction bonds

Use subtraction bonds to subtract large numbers, e.g. $8 - 3 = 5$
$80 - 30 = 50$

Odd & even numbers

Adding odd and even numbers always makes an odd number:
$3 + 8 = 11$

Adding two odd numbers always makes an even number:
$3 + 5 = 8$

Subtracting two odd numbers always makes an even number:
$9 - 3 = 6$

Subtracting odd and even numbers always makes an odd number:
$12 - 3 = 9$
$15 - 4 = 11$

Learning outcomes for UNIT 3

✓ knows addition and subtraction bonds to 20
✓ knows addition and subtraction are inverses
✓ extends addition and subtraction bonds to large numbers
✓ finds differences
✓ uses quick method of addition and subtraction e.g. +9 and −9
✓ knows and uses language of addition and subtraction
✓ uses addition and subtraction bonds in measurement contexts
✓ knows addition is commutative $8 + 3 = 3 + 8$
✓ uses brackets in simple calculations
✓ solves missing number problems
✓ totals several small numbers

3.1

Addition Bonds to 20

Write the answers. Check them.

1. 6 + 5	**4.** 8 + 9	**7.** 9 + 9	**10.** 15 + 3	**13.** 3 + 14
2. 7 + 9	**5.** 7 + 4	**8.** 8 + 7	**11.** 17 + 2	**14.** 4 + 13
3. 6 + 6	**6.** 8 + 8	**9.** 13 + 4	**12.** 12 + 8	**15.** 5 + 14

A

Write the missing numbers.

1. $9 + 4 = \square$ **4.** $4 + \square = 9$ **7.** $\square + 8 = 17$ **10.** $8 + 9 = \square$

2. $\square + 7 = 13$ **5.** $\square + 7 = 14$ **8.** $4 + \square = 11$ **11.** $\square + 9 = 18$

3. $5 + \square = 14$ **6.** $6 + 9 = \square$ **9.** $\square + 5 = 13$ **12.** $8 + \square = 15$

B

Look at the number machine.
Copy and complete the tables.

→ In | +5 |Out →

1.

In	9		10		3
Out		9		13	

2.

In	3		8		7
Out		12		17	

3.

In	2		6		9
Out		14		20	

C

Write the missing amounts.

1. $10p + \square = 15p$ **4.** $6p + \square = 20p$ **7.** $6p + 4p + \square = 16p$

2. $8p + \square = 20p$ **5.** $8p + \square = 17p$ **8.** $3p + 2p + \square = 17p$

3. $4p + \square = 16p$ **6.** $5p + 3p + \square = 20p$ **9.** $4p + 7p + \square = 20p$

D

Write the answers.

1. Total 7, 4 and 5.

2. Add together 3, 6 and 8.

3. Find the sum of 4, 2 and 10.

4. Double 6 then add 4.

5. Find 3 more than the sum of 5 and 6.

6. Find 5 more than double 4.

7. Find 7 more than 6.

8. Find two odd numbers less than 10 which total 18.

9. Find two different even numbers less than 10 which total 12.

10. Find how many more is 17 than 12.

3.2 Subtraction Facts to 20

Write the answers. Check them.

1. 14 – 8	5. 19 – 9	9. 16 – 8	13. 15 – 3	17. 13 – 3
2. 15 – 7	6. 14 – 7	10. 15 – 6	14. 19 – 1	18. 17 – 4
3. 17 – 8	7. 18 – 9	11. 12 – 2	15. 19 – 4	19. 16 – 3
4. 13 – 5	8. 12 – 4	12. 20 – 6	16. 16 – 5	20. 20 – 3

A

Write the answers.

1. $16 \xrightarrow{-9} \square$

2. $13 \xrightarrow{-10} \square$

3. $12 \xrightarrow{-8} \square$

4. $17 \xrightarrow{-8} \square$

5. $12 \xrightarrow{-3} \square$

6. $\square \xrightarrow{-9} 4$

7. $\square \xrightarrow{-9} 9$

8. $\square \xrightarrow{-4} 8$

9. $\square \xrightarrow{-8} 8$

10. $\square \xrightarrow{-9} 5$

11. $13 \xrightarrow{-\square} 5$

12. $15 \xrightarrow{-\square} 10$

13. $17 \xrightarrow{-\square} 6$

14. $12 \xrightarrow{-\square} 7$

15. $14 \xrightarrow{-\square} 6$

B

Write the difference between each pair of numbers.

1. 14 3	5. 17 4	9. 13 18	13. 16 9	17. 6 14
2. 18 2	6. 16 14	10. 11 20	14. 18 10	18. 8 15
3. 4 15	7. 20 12	11. 9 4	15. 14 5	19. 16 7
4. 3 13	8. 12 17	12. 8 17	16. 15 9	20. 7 17

C

1. Subtract 7 from 18.

2. Take 4 from 12.

3. 15 minus 4.

4. 20 subtract 6.

5. 13 take away 6.

6. What is 4 less than 15?

7. What is 6 fewer than 20?

8. The difference between 6 and 19.

9. What is 11 minus 4?

10. What is 11 take away 9?

11. What is 6 less than 19?

12. 18 minus 7.

Addition and Subtraction Facts to 20

A

Copy and complete each number chain.

1. $10 \xrightarrow{+5}$ 🧁 $\xrightarrow{-3}$ 🧁 $\xrightarrow{-2}$ 🧁 $\xrightarrow{+6}$ 🧁

2. $20 \xrightarrow{-3}$ 🧁 $\xrightarrow{-10}$ 🧁 $\xrightarrow{+5}$ 🧁 $\xrightarrow{+2}$ 🧁

3. $8 \xrightarrow{+9}$ 🧁 $\xrightarrow{-3}$ 🧁 $\xrightarrow{+4}$ 🧁 $\xrightarrow{-5}$ 🧁

4. $12 \xrightarrow{-8}$ 🧁 $\xrightarrow{-4}$ 🧁 $\xrightarrow{+7}$ 🧁 $\xrightarrow{+5}$ 🧁

5. $19 \xrightarrow{+1}$ 🧁 $\xrightarrow{-10}$ 🧁 $\xrightarrow{+3}$ 🧁 $\xrightarrow{-7}$ 🧁

B

Write what each arrow means.

1. 8 ▷━● 12

2. 5 ▷━● 17

3. 20 ▷━● 6

4. 4 ▷━● 17

5. 16 ▷━● 2

6. 12 ▷━● 3

7. 11 ▷━● 14

8. 17 ▷━● 13

9. 20 ▷━● 16

10. 19 ▷━● 6

11. 15 ▷━● 14

12. 17 ▷━● 6

13. 8 ▷━● 15

14. 7 ▷━● 19

15. 16 ▷━● 0

16. 4 ▷━● 16

17. 18 ▷━● 2

18. 20 ▷━● 1

Addition and Subtraction Facts to 20

C ....

Look at the price labels and write the change from 20p.

1. 8p + 7p

2. 10p + 3p

3. 6p + 4p

4. 1p + 3p

5. 6p + 6p

6. 17p + 1p

7. 4p + 1p

8. 13p + 2p

9. 6p + 12p

10. 5p + 5p

11. 3p + 4p

12. 7p + 3p

13. 11p + 9p

14. 2p + 2p

15. 5p + 9p

D ....

Work out the brackets first to answer the sums.

1. $17 - (9 + 3)$

2. $14 - (6 + 6)$

3. $13 - (10 + 3)$

4. $19 - (5 + 5)$

5. $16 - (8 + 2)$

6. $20 - (13 - 2)$

7. $15 - (9 - 6)$

8. $18 - (8 - 3)$

9. $17 - (10 - 3)$

10. $16 - (20 - 4)$

11. $(6 + 8) + 3$

12. $(20 - 3) + 2$

13. $(17 - 2) - 9$

14. $(9 + 9) - 10$

15. $(8 + 5) + 4$

16. $(19 - 8) - 3$

17. $(3 + 10) - 4$

18. $(16 - 6) + 10$

E ....

Look for number pairs which make 10 and write the answers to the sums.

1. $5 + 9 + 5$

2. $7 + 2 + 8$

3. $6 + 8 + 4$

4. $7 + 6 + 3$

5. $9 + 8 + 1$

6. $16 - 3 - 6$

7. $15 - 9 - 5$

8. $19 - 4 - 9$

9. $17 - 3 - 7$

10. $18 - 8 - 6$

11. $8 + 7 + 2 + 3$

12. $5 + 7 + 3 + 5$

13. $4 + 2 + 6 + 3$

14. $9 + 3 + 6 + 1$

15. $5 + 8 + 3 + 2$

16. $2 + 7 + 3 + 3$

17. $6 + 1 + 4 + 3$

18. $8 + 4 + 5 + 2$

Using Addition and Subtraction Facts to 20

Key Skills ✔

Write the answers. Check them.

1. 8 + 3	5. 3 + 9	9. 5 + 5	13. 14 – 9	17. 9 – 4
2. 6 + 6	6. 7 + 7	10. 7 + 2	14. 13 – 5	18. 12 – 9
3. 9 + 8	7. 4 + 3	11. 11 – 3	15. 12 – 6	19. 8 – 3
4. 4 + 7	8. 8 + 2	12. 17 – 7	16. 10 – 5	20. 17 – 8

A

Write the answers.

1. 40 + 30	5. 50 + 50	9. 60 + 40	13. 180 – 90	17. 170 – 30
2. 80 + 20	6. 80 + 80	10. 90 + 80	14. 150 – 70	18. 150 – 50
3. 50 + 80	7. 50 + 60	11. 120 – 60	15. 130 – 80	19. 110 – 80
4. 90 + 60	8. 70 + 70	12. 150 – 10	16. 160 – 80	20. 120 – 70

B

Write the missing numbers.

1. ◯ + 30 = 100	5. ◯ + 50 = 100	9. 60 + ◯ = 100	13. 100 – ◯ = 50
2. ◯ + 20 = 100	6. 40 + ◯ = 100	10. 70 + ◯ = 100	14. 100 – ◯ = 40
3. ◯ + 10 = 100	7. 90 + ◯ = 100	11. 100 – ◯ = 60	15. 100 – ◯ = 10
4. ◯ + 80 = 100	8. 30 + ◯ = 100	12. 100 – ◯ = 80	16. 100 – ◯ = 20

C

Make each total 1000.

1. 800 + 🐥	6. 🐥 + 400	11. 400 + 200 + 🐥
2. 500 + 🐥	7. 🐥 + 700	12. 🐥 + 100 + 700
3. 300 + 🐥	8. 🐥 + 900	13. 400 + 🐥 + 400
4. 200 + 🐥	9. 🐥 + 500	14. 🐥 + 700 + 100
5. 100 + 🐥	10. 🐥 + 600	15. 300 + 600 + 🐥

Problems Using Addition and Subtraction Bonds

Key Skills ✔

Write the answers. Check them.

1. 5 + 7	**6.** 12 – 4	**11.** (8 + 4) – 3
2. 9 + 4	**7.** 13 – 8	**12.** 15 – (6 + 3)
3. 8 + 3	**8.** 15 – 6	**13.** (14 – 7) + 4
4. 4 + 7	**9.** 16 – 7	**14.** 17 – (9 – 4)
5. 6 + 6	**10.** 14 – 5	**15.** (5 + 4) + 6

A

1. Two numbers have a difference of 8. The smaller number is 3. What is the larger number?
2. Two numbers added together make 19. One number is one more than the other. What are the two numbers?
3. What is the difference between the sum of 3 and 4 and the sum of 7 and 6?
4. How much more is the sum of 8 and 7 than the sum of 4 and 8?
5. What is the total of double 8 and half of 12?

B

1. Emily has £17 which is £3 more than Henry. How much has Henry?
2. Sunil has £3 which is £7 less than George. How much have they altogether?
3. Jan and Morgan have a total of £12. Morgan has £2 more than Jan. How much has Jan?
4. Tom has £10 and Jo has half as much. How much have they altogether?
5. Sally has £1 and Jordan has 40p. How much more has Sally?
6. William has 40p more than Kim. Kim has 30p.
   How much have they altogether?

C

Subtract each number from 100.

1. 20	**5.** 50
2. 80	**6.** 30
3. 60	**7.** 70
4. 100	**8.** 90

Subtract each number from 1000.

9. 10	**13.** 200
10. 40	**14.** 1000
11. 900	**15.** 600
12. 400	**16.** 700

Problems Using Addition and Subtraction Bonds

D ....

How many hours between these times?

	morning times			afternoon times			morning afternoon	

1. 4.00 am | 6.00 am   **6.** 1.00 pm | 6.00 pm   **11.** 10.00 am | 1.00 pm

2. 1.00 am | 6.00 am   **7.** 6.00 pm | 10.00 pm   **12.** 11.00 am | 4.00 pm

3. 3.00 am | 8.00 am   **8.** 5.00 pm | 8.00 pm   **13.** 9.00 am | 3.00 pm

4. 7.00 am | 11.00 am   **9.** 10.00 pm | 11.00 pm   **14.** 8.00 am | 2.00 pm

5. 9.00 am | 11.00 am   **10.** 3.00 pm | 9.00 pm   **15.** 5.00 am | 6.00 pm

E ....

1. Which three cards total 15?
2. Which two cards have an even total over 10?
3. Which two cards have an odd total over 10?
4. Which three cards have an odd total?
5. Which two cards have the largest difference?
6. Which three cards have a total of 16?

Summary for Unit 3

A

Write the answers.

1. 8 + 7
2. 10 + 4
3. 6 + 5
4. 8 + 5

5. Total 8, 4 and 6.
6. Double 3 then add 4.
7. Double 9 then subtract 3.
8. Add together 3, 5 and 7.

9. 5p + 7p
10. 10p + 4p
11. 15p + 2p
12. 3p + 17p

B

Write the answers.

1. 12 – 3
2. 15 – 6
3. 18 – 4
4. 20 – 3

Write the differences.

5. 10 4
6. 5 12
7. 20 7
8. 15 12

Write the change from 20p.

9. 6p
10. 8p
11. 13p
12. 15p

C

Write what each arrow means.

1. 8 ⟶ 12
2. 3 ⟶ 16
3. 12 ⟶ 4
4. 15 ⟶ 12

Answer the sums.

5. 15 – (4 + 6)
6. 13 + (10 – 4)
7. 8 + (8 + 2)
8. 16 – (10 – 3)

D

Write the answers.

1. 80 + 40
2. 60 + 50
3. 90 + 30
4. 20 + 50
5. 30 + 70

Write the answers.

6. 180 – 50
7. 150 – 30
8. 120 – 60
9. 130 – 90
10. 170 – 80

Write what needs to be added to make 100.

11. 70
12. 60
13. 80
14. 10

E

1. How many hours between these times? | 10.00 am | | 1.00 pm |
2. What is the total of £8, £3 and £6?
3. How much is left from £1 after spending 20p and 40p?

37

Addition of Numbers

Knowledge needed
✓ efficient use of addition facts to 20
✓ knowledge of place value

Helpful facts

Addition can be done in any order

It does not matter in which order you add numbers.
Choose the order you find easiest.
example
8 + 56 = 56 + 8
26 + 34 = 34 + 26

Knowing doubles

Knowing doubles can help you find other totals.
example
30 + 30 = 60
30 + 40 = 70

36 + 36 = 72
36 + 37 = 73

Number pairs which total 10

The number pairs which total 10 are very important. This can be extended to decades which total 100.

	decades
9,1	90,10
8,2	80,20
7,3	70,30
6,4	60,40
5,5	50,50

Quick methods

• Adding 9: – add 10 subtract 1
• Adding 19: – add 20 subtract 1
• Adding 99: – add 100 subtract 1
• Adding 999: – add 1000 subtract

Addition & subtraction are opposites

An addition sum can be checked by subtracting:

47 + 25 = 72

72 - 25 = 47

Breaking up numbers sometimes helps to add mentally

3   6 + 5   7

↓   ↓   ↓   ↓

(30 + 6) + (50 + 7)

add the tens then add the units

80 + 13 = 93

Adding the nearest decade number and adjusting

36 + 59

36 + [60 then − 1] = 95

54 + 72

54 + [70 then + 2] = 126

Learning outcomes for UNIT 4

✓ mentally adds pairs of decade numbers and hundred numbers

✓ doubles any 2-digit number

✓ knows complements to 100

✓ totals two or more 2-digit numbers

✓ totals pairs of 3-digit numbers

✓ totals in context of measure and money

✓ solves missing digit problems

✓ uses a range of mental methods for addition

✓ knows relationships between addition and subtraction

4.1

Quick Addition

A ....

Add 9 to each number.

1. 46	**4.** 98	**7.** 467	**10.** 586	**13.** 398	**16.** 1348
2. 39	**5.** 72	**8.** 208	**11.** 196	**14.** 695	**17.** 2694
3. 54	**6.** 136	**9.** 365	**12.** 294	**15.** 997	**18.** 1997

B ....

Add 19 to each number.

1. 37	**4.** 84	**7.** 308	**10.** 742	**13.** 488	**16.** 1425
2. 48	**5.** 75	**8.** 542	**11.** 684	**14.** 580	**17.** 3840
3. 69	**6.** 236	**9.** 630	**12.** 785	**15.** 386	**18.** 2182

C ....

Add 99 to each number.

1. 81	**4.** 71	**7.** 840	**10.** 710	**13.** 953	**16.** 1472
2. 67	**5.** 36	**8.** 390	**11.** 980	**14.** 975	**17.** 2054
3. 86	**6.** 460	**9.** 850	**12.** 964	**15.** 962	**18.** 3672

D ....

Add 11 to each number.

1. 156	**4.** 875	**7.** 569	**10.** 709	**13.** 899	**16.** 2649
2. 208	**5.** 793	**8.** 239	**11.** 299	**14.** 399	**17.** 1399
3. 346	**6.** 439	**9.** 489	**12.** 699	**15.** 889	**18.** 4079

E ....

Add 999 to each number.

1. 436	**4.** 396	**7.** 450	**10.** 810	**13.** 5356	**16.** 1200
2. 522	**5.** 751	**8.** 960	**11.** 2924	**14.** 4842	**17.** 6300
3. 688	**6.** 760	**9.** 620	**12.** 3468	**15.** 6105	**18.** 7400

Adding TU Mentally

A ....

Write the answers.

1. 46 + 23	**5.** 22 + 46	**9.** 13 + 52	**13.** 24 + 23	**17.** 15 + 72
2. 36 + 12	**6.** 50 + 21	**10.** 38 + 21	**14.** 32 + 43	**18.** 34 + 35
3. 15 + 60	**7.** 63 + 12	**11.** 36 + 23	**15.** 41 + 45	**19.** 26 + 22
4. 75 + 13	**8.** 14 + 23	**12.** 52 + 15	**16.** 36 + 22	**20.** 54 + 34

B ....

Double each number.

1. 34	**4.** 14	**7.** 35	**10.** 55	**13.** 26	**16.** 54
2. 21	**5.** 33	**8.** 15	**11.** 18	**14.** 37	**17.** 62
3. 43	**6.** 45	**9.** 25	**12.** 17	**15.** 29	**18.** 81

C ....

Each total is 100. Write the missing numbers.

1. 30 +    **4.** 80 +   **7.** 60 +   **10.** 90 +   **13.** 2 +   **16.** 4 +

2. 50 +   **5.** 40 +   **8.** 100 +   **11.** 0 +   **14.** 8 +   **17.** 1 +

3. 70 +   **6.** 20 +   **9.** 10 +   **12.** 5 +   **15.** 6 +   **18.** 7 +

D ....

Write what must be added to each number to make 100.

1. 45	**4.** 95	**7.** 76	**10.** 22	**13.** 81	**16.** 45
2. 15	**5.** 35	**8.** 39	**11.** 52	**14.** 19	**17.** 64
3. 75	**6.** 43	**9.** 89	**12.** 63	**15.** 44	**18.** 88

E ....

Add these near doubles.

1. 13 14	**3.** 16 15	**5.** 15 14	**7.** 24 23	**9.** 25 24
2. 17 18	**4.** 18 19	**6.** 17 16	**8.** 21 22	**10.** 23 22

(4.3)

Adding TU and TU

Write the answers. Check them.

1. 9 + 7	**3.** 3 + 8	**5.** 9 + 6	**7.** 50 + 60	**9.** 30 + 50
2. 4 + 7	**4.** 6 + 4	**6.** 30 + 40	**8.** 80 + 80	**10.** 70 + 70

A

1. 24 + 57	**5.** 34 + 26	**9.** 36 + 47	**13.** 69 + 72	**17.** 68 + 75
2. 36 + 25	**6.** 47 + 47	**10.** 26 + 59	**14.** 83 + 41	**18.** 73 + 74
3. 19 + 34	**7.** 54 + 18	**11.** 52 + 58	**15.** 59 + 49	**19.** 69 + 84
4. 18 + 25	**8.** 17 + 48	**12.** 64 + 57	**16.** 75 + 75	**20.** 92 + 89

B

Find the missing digits and write the sums.

1.
```
   26
+ 3●
────
   63
```

3.
```
  ●5
+ 18
────
  43
```

5.
```
   2●
+ 67
────
  ●2
```

7.
```
  ●4
+ 3●
────
  82
```

9.
```
   3●
+ 37
────
  ●3
```

2.
```
   4●
+ 47
────
   94
```

4.
```
   46
+ ●8
────
   84
```

6.
```
   56
+ ●●
────
   90
```

8.
```
   39
+ ●7
────
   5●
```

10.
```
   ●●
+ 26
────
   74
```

C

Add numbers in adjacent tins to find the number above.

1.

14 18 15

3.
19 26 22

5.

32 26 24

7.

34 28 29

9.
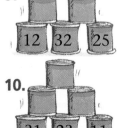
12 32 25

2.
23 16 24

4.

35 17 24

6.
23 28 25

8.
24 25 26

10.
31 23 11

42

4.4

Adding TU Problems

Key Skills ✔

Write the answers. Check them.

1. 45 + 26   **3.** 18 + 46   **5.** 42 + 29   **7.** 25 + 46   **9.** 84 + 23

2. 38 + 27   **4.** 28 + 36   **6.** 46 + 28   **8.** 36 + 52   **10.** 75 + 48

A

Copy and complete the tables.

1.

+	18		28
17			
	37		
24	48		

2.

+			28
22	46		
27		52	
			57

3.

+	25		
	58		71
27		46	
35			

B

The number in the purse is the total of two consecutive numbers.
Write the numbers.

1. 33   +   **3.** 53   +   **5.** 65   +   **7.** 75   +   **9.** 99   +

2. 111   +   **4.** 33   +   **6.** 143   +   **8.** 125   +   **10.** 161   +

C

Find each total. Write a sum.

1. 26, 34 and 27   **6.** 24p, 22p and 38p   **11.** 36 cm, 84 cm and 23 cm

2. 17, 18 and 34   **7.** 53p, 27p and 46p   **12.** 47 cm, 28 cm and 56 cm

3. 16, 25 and 38   **8.** 25p, 37p and 34p   **13.** 36 cm, 36 cm and 41 cm

4. 14, 27 and 46   **9.** 45p, 55p and 74p   **14.** 59 cm, 16 cm and 20 cm

5. 28, 32 and 44   **10.** 63p, 28p and 54p   **15.** 82 cm, 64 cm and 32 cm

Adding TU Problems

D ....

Find pairs which total 1 metre.
Write each pair as a sum.

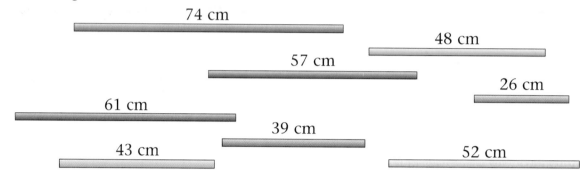

74 cm

48 cm

57 cm

26 cm

61 cm

39 cm

43 cm

52 cm

E ....

Which numbers go in each shape?
Shapes which are the same have the same number.

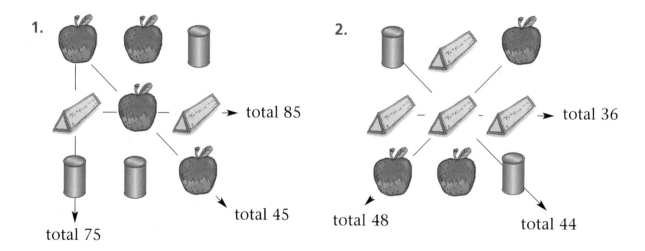

1.

total 85

total 45

total 75

2.

total 36

total 48

total 44

4.5

Adding HTU and TU

Write the answers. Check them.

1. 8 + 7	3. 6 + 4	5. 6 + 7	7. 70 + 70	9. 60 + 50
2. 9 + 9	4. 3 + 8	6. 40 + 50	8. 90 + 80	10. 70 + 90

A

1. 129 + 58	3. 235 + 47	5. 452 + 38	7. 427 + 27	9. 736 + 54
2. 108 + 79	4. 314 + 58	6. 504 + 87	8. 384 + 18	10. 639 + 25

B

1. 177 + 86	3. 437 + 94	5. 456 + 79	7. 493 + 98	9. 828 + 97
2. 236 + 94	4. 507 + 98	6. 368 + 59	8. 657 + 57	10. 777 + 55

C

Add 75 to these.		Add 50 to these.		Add 99 to these.		Add 38 to these.	
1. 175	3. 377	5. 480	7. 374	9. 176	11. 740	13. 195	15. 762
2. 265	4. 496	6. 685	8. 496	10. 497	12. 481	14. 472	16. 655

D

Add 40p to these.	Add 55p to these.	Add 68p to these.	Add 99p to these.
1. £2.60	6. £3.75	11. £1.26	16. £4.50
2. £3.50	7. £2.85	12. £2.35	17. £6.25
3. £5.90	8. £4.35	13. £4.94	18. £1.36
4. £1.80	9. £1.95	14. £3.75	19. £3.65
5. £3.70	10. £5.65	15. £6.99	20. £7.88

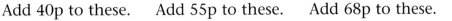

4.6

Adding with HTU

A

1. 400 + 300
2. 200 + 600
3. 300 + 500
4. 300 + 100
5. 500 + 500
6. 400 + 500
7. 300 + 400
8. 600 + 300
9. 500 + 300
10. 400 + 200
11. 600 + 200
12. 300 + 700

B

Add these near doubles.

1. 150 + 160
2. 230 + 220
3. 110 + 120
4. 120 + 130
5. 250 + 260
6. 330 + 340
7. 130 + 140
8. 320 + 330
9. 210 + 220
10. 240 + 250
11. 340 + 350
12. 180 + 170

C

Each total is 500. Write the missing number.

1. 450
2. 150
3. 250
4. 225
5. 125
6. 375
7. 475
8. 425
9. 325
10. 105
11. 315
12. 245
13. 165
14. 375
15. 465

D

Double each number.

1. 150
2. 650
3. 850
4. 750
5. 450
6. 950
7. 250
8. 320
9. 430
10. 370
11. 180
12. 410
13. 470
14. 560
15. 390

E

1. Sunil has 238 stickers.
   He collects 96 more.
   How many has he now?
2. Lucy has 57 stickers.
   Her brother has twice as many.
   How many have they altogether?
3. Neil has half as many stickers as Emma.
   Emma has 150 stickers.
   How many have they altogether?
4. Vicki has 150 stickers.
   Charlie has 160 stickers.
   What is the total of their stickers?

Addition Problems in Measurement

A ....

Calculate the perimeter of each shape.

1.

3. 60 cm

5. 74 cm

7. 16 cm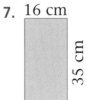

2.

4. 80 cm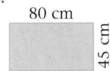

6. 38 cm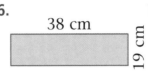

8.

B ....

Write the weight on each scale. Write the totals for each pair.

1.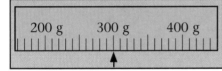

2.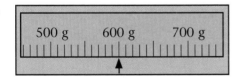

3.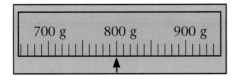

Addition Problems in Measurement

C ....

Write how much is in each container. Write the totals for each pair.

1.
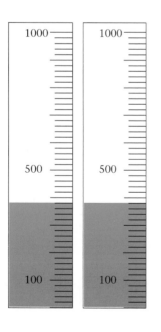

3.
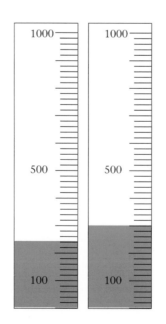

5.
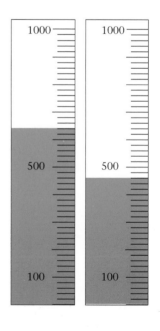

2.
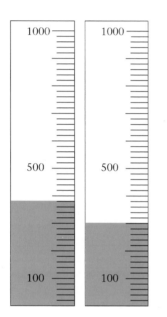

4.
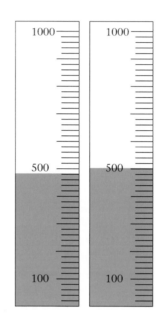

6.
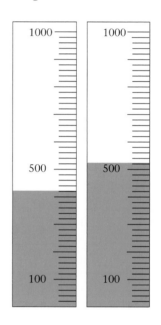

Summary for Unit 4

Ⓐ

Add 9.
1. 98
2. 245
3. 872
4. 1656

Add 99.
5. 75
6. 328
7. 964
8. 3245

Add 999.
9. 68
10. 347
11. 592
12. 1542

Add 999.
13. 45
14. 264
15. 889
16. 3207

Ⓑ

Total.
1. 27 and 32
2. 23 and 45
3. 34 and 34
4. 51 and 37

Double.
5. 45
6. 85
7. 86
8. 96

Make 100.
9. 30 + ☐
10. 70 + ☐
11. 55 + ☐
12. 65 + ☐

Make 100.
13. 8 + ☐
14. 13 + ☐
15. 46 + ☐
16. 82 + ☐

Ⓒ

1. 36
   + 48

2. 29
   + 57

3. 28
   + 28

4. 56
   + 29

5. 58
   + 65

6. 73
   + 37

7. 84
   + 79

8. 68
   + 56

Ⓓ

Add.
1. 236
   + 54

2. 435
   + 68

Double.
3. 450
4. 175

Add 99.
5. 243
6. 378

Add 50p.
7. £4.80
8. £1.90

Ⓔ

Write the perimeter.
1.

28 cm

19 cm

Write the total capacity.
2. ml 1000 + 500 + 100
3. ml 1000 + 300 + 100

Write the total weight.
4. kg 100 + 200 + 300 + 400
5. kg 500 + 600 + 700 + 800

Knowledge needed
✓ efficient use of subtraction facts to 10
✓ knowledge of place value

Subtraction of Numbers

Helpful facts

Quick methods
- **Subtracting 9:** $54 - 9 = 45$
  subtract 10 add 1
- **Subtracting 99:** $378 - 99 = 279$
  subtract 100 add 1
- **Subtracting 19:** $164 - 19 = 145$
  subtract 20 add 1

Difference
To find the difference   38   95
between two numbers, $95 - 38 = 57$
subtract them.   ← difference

Subtraction & addition are opposites
A subtraction sum can be $94 - 28 = 66$
checked by adding: $66 + 28 = 94$

Brackets
Work out the sum in $70 - (3 \times 7)$
the brackets first: ← work out first
                             $70 - 21 = 49$

Subtracting the nearest decade and adjusting
$87 - 39$ $73 - 24$
$87 - [40 + 1] = 48$ $73 - [20 - 4] = 49$

Breaking up numbers sometimes helps with mental subtraction

84 – 36

↓

84 – 30 – 6

= 54 – 6

= 48

When subtracting close numbers, count on or back

312 – 308 = 4

count on from 308 or count back from 312

Learning outcomes for UNIT 5

✓ uses quick methods for subtracting e.g. – 9, – 99

✓ finds differences between pairs of numbers

✓ finds complements to 100

✓ subtracts any pair of 2-digit numbers

✓ subtracts in the context of money and measurement

✓ solves missing number problems

✓ extends subtraction facts to working with larger numbers

✓ subtracts any 2-digit number from a 3-digit number

✓ knows relationships between addition and subtraction

✓ uses a range of mental methods for subtraction

5.1

Quick Methods of Subtraction

A

Subtract 9 from each number. Write the answers.

1. 42	**5.** 94	**9.** 377	**13.** 405	**17.** 2346
2. 56	**6.** 136	**10.** 450	**14.** 406	**18.** 1074
3. 75	**7.** 241	**11.** 203	**15.** 304	**19.** 3558
4. 68	**8.** 163	**12.** 108	**16.** 1425	**20.** 1623

B

The arrow represents –9. Write the missing numbers.

1. 135 ⟶ ⚽   **4.** 317 ⟶ ⚽   **7.** ⚽ ⟶ 145   **10.** ⚽ ⟶ 439

2. 208 ⟶ ⚽   **5.** 192 ⟶ ⚽   **8.** ⚽ ⟶ 341   **11.** ⚽ ⟶ 301

3. 454 ⟶ ⚽   **6.** ⚽ ⟶ 122   **9.** ⚽ ⟶ 426   **12.** 199 ⟶ ⚽

C

Put these numbers into the function machine.
Write which numbers leave.

⟶ In | –99 | Out ⟶

1. 434	**3.** 168	**5.** 470	**7.** 4223	**9.** 5691
2. 286	**4.** 385	**6.** 741	**8.** 8376	**10.** 6934

D

Write the answers.

1. 48 – 9	**4.** 86 – 49	**7.** 194 – 49	**10.** 427 – 31
2. 57 – 19	**5.** 75 – 39	**8.** 307 – 99	**11.** 562 – 51
3. 84 – 29	**6.** 236 – 9	**9.** 208 – 41	**12.** 324 – 31

E

Write how much change from £20.

1. £5.99	**4.** £1.99	**7.** £9.99	**10.** £4.49	**13.** £15.49
2. £3.99	**5.** £19.99	**8.** £5.49	**11.** £11.49	**14.** £10.49
3. £10.99	**6.** £4.99	**9.** £1.49	**12.** £18.49	**15.** £17.49

5.2

Mental Subtraction of TU

Key Skills ✔

Write the answers. Check them.

1. 9 – 4	**4.** 6 – 5	**7.** 70 – 30	**10.** 90 – 70	**13.** 80 – 1
2. 8 – 3	**5.** 4 – 4	**8.** 60 – 10	**11.** 20 – 6	**14.** 70 – 4
3. 7 – 0	**6.** 50 – 20	**9.** 40 – 20	**12.** 30 – 4	**15.** 50 – 7

A

Write the answers.

1. 47 – 23	**4.** 46 – 16	**7.** 86 – 40	**10.** 59 – 48	**13.** 85 – 73
2. 64 – 31	**5.** 35 – 24	**8.** 75 – 51	**11.** 96 – 35	**14.** 53 – 22
3. 39 – 15	**6.** 59 – 35	**9.** 66 – 32	**12.** 32 – 10	**15.** 77 – 67

B

Subtract each number from 100.

1. 40	**4.** 80	**7.** 75	**10.** 95	**13.** 22
2. 30	**5.** 60	**8.** 25	**11.** 54	**14.** 41
3. 70	**6.** 55	**9.** 45	**12.** 36	**15.** 57

C

Write the difference between each pair of numbers.

1. 40 17	**5.** 80 27	**9.** 50 26	**13.** 52 80	**17.** 13 30
2. 23 50	**6.** 90 46	**10.** 34 70	**14.** 80 37	**18.** 80 79
3. 19 70	**7.** 60 57	**11.** 70 64	**15.** 16 50	**19.** 45 70
4. 50 38	**8.** 14 30	**12.** 60 17	**16.** 50 12	**20.** 60 35

D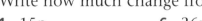

Write how much change from 50p

Write how much change from £1

1. 15p	**6.** 36p	**11.** 30p	**16.** 27p
2. 35p	**7.** 47p	**12.** 60p	**17.** 99p
3. 45p	**8.** 21p	**13.** 35p	**18.** 72p
4. 7p	**9.** 32p	**14.** 55p	**19.** 34p
5. 19p	**10.** 49p	**15.** 75p	**20.** 61p

5.3

Subtracting TU

Write the answers. Check them.

1. 13 – 8	**3.** 12 – 4	**5.** 16 – 9	**7.** 30 – 10	**9.** 80 – 20
2. 15 – 7	**4.** 11 – 9	**6.** 60 – 40	**8.** 70 – 50	**10.** 70 – 60

Ⓐ ....

1. 56 – 28	**5.** 43 – 18	**9.** 44 – 15	**13.** 63 – 36	**17.** 84 – 67
2. 47 – 38	**6.** 61 – 37	**10.** 78 – 39	**14.** 91 – 57	**18.** 65 – 36
3. 70 – 47	**7.** 72 – 48	**11.** 54 – 39	**15.** 71 – 68	**19.** 38 – 29
4. 81 – 25	**8.** 45 – 28	**12.** 80 – 41	**16.** 68 – 49	**20.** 40 – 17

Ⓑ ....

Write the missing digits.

1.
```
  8◯
– 45
────
  37
```
3.
```
  91
– 7◯
────
  17
```
5.
```
  74
– 3◯
────
  36
```
7.
```
  5◯
– 16
────
 ◯4
```
9.
```
 ◯8
– 7◯
────
  12
```

2.
```
  5◯
– 39
────
  17
```
4.
```
  80
– 5◯
────
  25
```
6.
```
  4◯
– 18
────
 ◯6
```
8.
```
 ◯0
– 4◯
────
  46
```
10.
```
 ◯2
– 2◯
────
  35
```

Ⓒ ....

1. Subtract 56 from 80.	**5.** What is 23 less than 41?
2. Take away 18 from 49.	**7.** What is 40 minus 17?
3. 74 minus 38.	**7.** How many less than 50 is 13?
4. Subtract 93 – 58.	**8.** What is 63 subtract 26?

Ⓓ ....

Write the remainders.

	Price.	Money given.
1.	72p	50p 20p 5p
2.	85p	50p 50p
3.	18p	50p

	Size of wood.	Length cut off.
4.	74 cm	38 cm
5.	36 cm	19 cm
6.	90 cm	62 cm

5.4

Number Differences

A

Write the differences between these close numbers.

1. 41 48	**4.** 96 102	**7.** 236 241	**10.** 463 458	**13.** 600 593
2. 58 63	**5.** 111 108	**8.** 308 312	**11.** 700 694	**14.** 400 392
3. 71 67	**6.** 156 160	**9.** 299 301	**12.** 891 900	**15.** 896 900

B

Write the difference between these close numbers.

1. 1000 997	**4.** 8000 7995	**7.** 8997 9000	**10.** 5998 6000	**13.** 4996 5001
2. 1994 2000	**5.** 6998 7000	**8.** 2992 3000	**11.** 1004 996	**14.** 4005 3997
3. 3998 4000	**6.** 2000 1999	**9.** 5000 4993	**12.** 1998 2004	**15.** 2991 3008

C

The number in the square is the difference between the two numbers. Write the missing numbers.

e.g. 57 ◄─ 8 ─► 49

1. 71 ◄─ ☐ ─► 36

2. 43 ◄─ ☐ ─► 18

3. 82 ◄─ ☐ ─► 55

4. 81 ◄─ 28 ─► ☐

5. 37 ◄─ 18 ─► ☐

6. 54 ◄─ 17 ─► ☐

7. ☐ ◄─ 39 ─► 32

8. ☐ ◄─ 27 ─► 46

9. ☐ ◄─ 28 ─► 51

D

Write the missing numbers.

1. 27 + ⬤ = 34	**4.** 127 + ⬤ = 132	**7.** 1246 + ⬤ = 1250
2. 38 + ⬤ = 42	**5.** 148 + ⬤ = 151	**8.** 2059 + ⬤ = 2062
3. 54 + ⬤ = 62	**6.** 166 + ⬤ = 175	**9.** 3408 + ⬤ = 3413

E

1. William has 34p. Hayley has 72p. How much less has William?
2. Damien has 181 stamps. Lucy has 6 fewer stamps. How many has Lucy?
3. Mr Kirk is 74 years old. His brother is 65 years old. How much older is Mr Kirk than his brother?

5.5

Subtracting HTU and TU with One Exchange

Write the answers. Check them.

1. 12 – 4	**3.** 10 – 6	**5.** 12 – 8	**7.** 60 – 30	**9.** 90 – 70
2. 15 – 9	**4.** 11 – 7	**6.** 50 – 30	**8.** 80 – 40	**10.** 90 – 10

Ⓐ

1. 143 – 28	**4.** 242 – 38	**7.** 475 – 59	**10.** 890 – 43
2. 280 – 54	**5.** 684 – 45	**8.** 655 – 46	**11.** 662 – 57
3. 352 – 39	**6.** 560 – 31	**9.** 783 – 67	**12.** 472 – 46

Ⓑ

1. 245 – 72	**4.** 436 – 51	**7.** 478 – 94	**10.** 425 – 44
2. 318 – 43	**5.** 513 – 62	**8.** 506 – 62	**11.** 138 – 72
3. 304 – 62	**6.** 346 – 73	**9.** 814 – 75	**12.** 274 – 93

Ⓒ

Subtract:	Which number is:	What is the difference between:
1. 38 from 346	**5.** 29 less than 257	**9.** 374 and 47
2. 74 from 408	**6.** 35 less than 360	**10.** 75 and 419
3. 48 from 277	**7.** 78 less than 592	**11.** 82 and 372
4. 72 from 584	**8.** 92 less than 434	**12.** 936 and 28

Ⓓ

Complete these number chains and check that the last number is true.

1. 850 $\xrightarrow{-28}$ ☐ $\xrightarrow{-17}$ ☐ $\xrightarrow{-72}$ ☐ $\xrightarrow{-61}$ 672

2. 429 $\xrightarrow{-32}$ ☐ $\xrightarrow{-29}$ ☐ $\xrightarrow{-85}$ ☐ $\xrightarrow{-91}$ 192

5.6

Subtracting HTU and TU with Exchange

A

1. 324
− 76

3. 413
− 65

5. 433
− 68

7. 632
− 75

2. 506
− 79

4. 240
− 78

6. 712
− 85

8. 444
− 96

B

1. 500 − 46
2. 400 − 37
3. 200 − 72

4. 700 − 42
5. 300 − 62
6. 500 − 77

7. 700 − 79
8. 300 − 42
9. 800 − 86

10. 900 − 64
11. 400 − 81
12. 500 − 72

C

Look at these number cards.

760   75   300

800   24   48

A 760
B 75
C 300
D 800
E 24
F 48

1. What is the difference between C and F?
2. Which card is 276 less than C?
3. What is A subtract B?
4. What is the difference between D and F?
5. What is C subtract E?

D

Write the missing digits.

1. 43◯
− 65
367

3. 7◯0
− 62
658

5. 62◯
− 83
540

7. 43◯
− ◯8
338

2. 50◯
− 142
358

4. 2◯4
− 22
192

6. 5◯3
− 29
554

8. 70◯
− ◯2
652

Subtraction Problems

A

1. $130 - (5 \times 7)$
2. $250 - (3 \times 3)$
3. $400 - (9 \times 5)$
4. $350 - (2 \times 8)$

5. $500 - (7 \times 2)$
6. $300 - (20 + 4)$
7. $450 - (60 + 8)$
8. $550 - (80 + 9)$

9. $200 - (50 + 3)$
10. $600 - (70 + 5)$
11. $200 - (40 - 5)$
12. $150 - (30 - 8)$

13. $400 - (20 - 7)$
14. $600 - (90 - 2)$
15. $700 - (70 - 4)$
16. $800 - (50 - 3)$

B

Choose from the cards to make each sum true.

0   1   5   2   8

1.
   46

2.
   31

3.
   31

4.
   13

5.
   32

6.
   78

7.
   18

8.
   44

C

1. 🏈 $- 49 = 72$
2. 🏈 $- 58 = 72$
3. $132 - $ 🏈 $= 72$
4. $116 - $ 🏈 $= 72$

5. 🏈 $- 54 = 99$
6. $160 - $ 🏈 $= 99$
7. $155 - $ 🏈 $= 99$
8. $175 - $ 🏈 $= 99$

9. 🏈 $- 58 = 75$
10. $136 - $ 🏈 $= 75$
11. $151 - $ 🏈 $= 75$
12. $99 - $ 🏈 $= 75$

Summary for Unit 5

A

Subtract 9 from:
1. 56
2. 83
3. 146
4. 307

Subtract 99 from:
5. 430
6. 518
7. 324
8. 865

Change from £10:
9. £1.99
10. £3.99
11. £6.99
12. £2.49

B

Write the answers.
1. 54 – 23
2. 87 – 45
3. 65 – 21
4. 96 – 34

Subtract from 100.
5. 45
6. 62
7. 37
8. 51

Number difference.
9. 50 27
10. 42 80
11. 36 70
12. 60 47

C

1. 51 – 36
2. 45 – 27
3. 61 – 43
4. 80 – 58

5. Subtract 43 from 71.
6. Take 19 from 81.
7. 50 minus 23.
8. 61 take away 34.

9. 80p – 28p
10. 70p – 46p
11. 35p – 27p
12. 90p – 76p

D

1. 476
   – 28

2. 635
   – 27

3. 480
   – 66

4. 318
   – 74

5. 206
   – 42

6. 516
   – 75

7. 314
   – 68

8. 218
   – 89

E

Find the difference.
1. 158 and 164
2. 637 and 742
3. 1214 and 1221

Write the answer.
4. $400 - (3 \times 3)$
5. $300 - (7 \times 2)$
6. $600 - (5 \times 9)$

Missing number.
7. $42 + \boxed{} = 73$
8. $58 + \boxed{} = 95$
9. $121 - \boxed{} = 86$

Knowledge needed
✓ addition facts
✓ tables for 2, 5 and 10

Helpful facts

Anyway round
The order of multiplication does not matter:

$3 \times 8 = 8 \times 3$ $7 \times 9 = 9 \times 7$

Endings
Multiplying with 2s
all the answers will be even:

$2 \times 7 = 14$ $9 \times 2 = 18$

Multiplying with 5s
all the answers will end in 5 or 0:

$5 \times 6 = 30$ $9 \times 5 = 45$

Multiplying with 10s
all the answers will end in 0:

$10 \times 3 = 30$ $7 \times 10 = 70$

Brackets
Work out the sum in the brackets first:

$(7 \times 6) - 3$

↖ work out first

$42 - 3 = 39$

Multiplying decade numbers
Multiply significant numbers first then adjust for the tens:

multiply first

↓   ↓

$30 \times 60 = 1800$

Some quick methods
• Multiplying by 5, multiply by 10 then halve:

9×5

$= \frac{1}{2}$ of $90 = 45$

• Multiplying by 4, double then double again:

7×4

double $7 = 14$

double $14 = 28$

• Multiplying by 6, multiply by 3 then double:

8×6

double $(8 \times 3) = 48$

Multiplication & division are opposite
Division is the opposite of multiplication:

$9 \times 8 = 72$

$72 \div 8 = 9$

Multiplying TU

Either multiply tens first then units:

36 × 4

(30 × 4) + (6 × 4)

120 + 24 = 144

or multiply units first then tens:

(6 × 4) + (30 × 4)

24 + 120 = 144

Multiples

Multiples of a number can be exactly divided by that number:

Multiples of 5 ➤ 5, 10, 15, 20, 25, ...

Multiples of 9 ➤ 9, 18, 27, 36, ...

Multiples do not stop at 10x the number, they go on and on:

Multiples of 4 ➤ 36, 40, 44, 48, ...

Multiples of 7 ➤ 63, 70, 77, 84, ...

Learning outcomes for UNIT 6

✓ knows 2×, 5×, 10× tables by heart

✓ knows 3×, 4× tables by heart

✓ knows some of the 6×, 7×, 8×, 9× tables by heart

✓ knows multiplication is commutative 4 × 7 = 7 × 4

✓ recognises multiplication of numbers

✓ can double or halve numbers

✓ recognises multiplication and division are inverses

✓ solves missing number problems

✓ uses multiplication in context of money and measures

✓ multiplies 2-digit numbers by single digits

✓ can use quick methods for multiplication

✓ can multiply decade numbers by decade numbers

6.1

Multiplying by 2, 5 and 10

A

Write the answers.

1. 2 × 7	**5.** 7 × 2	**9.** 5 × 3	**13.** 7 × 5	**17.** 10 × 10	**21.** 10 × 3
2. 2 × 5	**6.** 10 × 2	**10.** 5 × 4	**14.** 5 × 5	**18.** 6 × 10	**22.** 10 × 4
3. 2 × 9	**7.** 6 × 2	**11.** 5 × 6	**15.** 8 × 5	**19.** 2 × 10	**23.** 10 × 5
4. 2 × 8	**8.** 3 × 2	**12.** 5 × 8	**16.** 10 × 5	**20.** 7 × 10	**24.** 10 × 9

B

Copy and complete the tables.

1. → In | ×2 | Out →

IN	7			9
OUT		16	12	

2. → In | ×5 | Out →

IN	8		6	
OUT		45		25

3. → In | ×10 | Out →

IN	5		9	
OUT		40		60

C

Work out the brackets first. Write the answers.

1. (5 × 5) + (4 × 5)
2. (2 × 9) + (7 × 2)
3. (2 × 8) + (10 × 3)

4. (10 × 10) – (3 × 10)
5. (6 × 10) – (10 × 3)
6. (9 × 5) – (2 × 9)

7. (3 × 4) + (10 × 8)
8. (7 × 2) – (2 × 6)
9. (5 × 7) + (5 × 3)

D

1. One book costs £5.
What would seven books cost?
2. Two books cost £6.
What would five books cost?
3. One book costs £2.
How many can be bought for £13?

4. There are 10 seeds in a row.
How many in 7 rows?
5. There are 50 seeds in a box.
There are 5 rows of seeds.
How many seeds in each row?
6. A pile of 2p coins is worth 16p.
How many 2p coins in the pile?

Multiplying by 3 and 4

A

1. 3×8	**4.** 10×3	**7.** 4×10	**10.** 4×4	**13.** 3×6	**16.** 8×3
2. 3×5	**5.** 4×3	**8.** 4×7	**11.** 4×9	**14.** 9×4	**17.** 7×4
3. 3×7	**6.** 5×3	**9.** 4×5	**12.** 6×4	**15.** 3×3	**18.** 3×4

B

Write two different multiplication sums for each total.

1. ☐ × ☐ 12 ☐ × ☐   **4.** ☐ × ☐ 16 ☐ × ☐   **7.** ☐ × ☐ 24 ☐ × ☐
2. ☐ × ☐ 20 ☐ × ☐   **5.** ☐ × ☐ 6 ☐ × ☐   **8.** ☐ × ☐ 30 ☐ × ☐
3. ☐ × ☐ 15 ☐ × ☐   **6.** ☐ × ☐ 40 ☐ × ☐   **9.** ☐ × ☐ 36 ☐ × ☐

C

Write the missing numbers.

1. $4 \times$ 🌼 $= 16$ **5.** 🌼 $\times 4 = 12$ **9.** $4 \times$ 🌼 $= 40$ **13.** $9 \times 4 =$ 🌼

2. $4 \times$ 🌼 $= 24$ **6.** 🌼 $\times 3 = 9$ **10.** 🌼 $\times 8 = 24$ **14.** $4 \times 60 =$ 🌼

3. $2 \times$ 🌼 $= 16$ **7.** 🌼 $\times 7 = 28$ **11.** $4 \times$ 🌼 $= 0$ **15.** $4 \times 90 =$ 🌼

4. $6 \times$ 🌼 $= 18$ **8.** 🌼 $\times 3 = 30$ **12.** 🌼 $\times 2 = 8$ **16.** $4 \times 300 =$ 🌼

D

Use your number facts to answer these.

1. 40×3	**4.** 3×70	**7.** 80×4	**10.** 4×60
2. 30×3	**5.** 3×20	**8.** 30×4	**11.** 4×90
3. 80×3	**6.** 3×50	**9.** 50×4	**12.** 4×700

E

1. What would 4 adults pay on Tuesday?
2. What would 7 adults pay on Saturday?
3. What would two children pay on Friday?
4. What would six children pay on Saturday?

Monday – Friday
Adults: £3
Saturday – Sunday
Adults: £4
Children half price

6.3

Multiplying by 6

A

1. 6 × 1
2. 6 × 5
3. 6 × 2
4. 6 × 7

5. 6 × 3
6. 6 × 4
7. 6 × 6
8. 6 × 10

9. 6 × 8
10. 6 × 9
11. 1 × 6
12. 2 × 6

13. 5 × 6
14. 4 × 6
15. 10 × 6
16. 3 × 6

17. 0 × 6
18. 9 × 6
19. 7 × 6
20. 8 × 6

B

Look at the number machine.
Copy and complete the tables.

1.

IN	6	9	5	10
OUT				

2.

IN				
OUT	48	24	42	54

3.

IN	3		6	
OUT		60		30

C

Multiply each number by 6.

0	3	10	5	8	2	9	4	7	6

Multiply each number by 3, then double.

1	5	10	15	4	9	7	3	8	6

D

Use your number facts to answer these.

1. 10 × 6
2. 20 × 6
3. 90 × 6
4. 70 × 6

5. 50 × 6
6. 80 × 6
7. 30 × 6
8. 100 × 6

9. 10 × 60
10. 50 × 60
11. 100 × 60
12. 30 × 60

13. 40 × 60
14. 60 × 60
15. 90 × 60
16. 70 × 60

E

1. 6 × 2 × 3
2. 2 × 6 × 5
3. 3 × 3 × 6
4. 2 × 6 × 4

5. 6 × 8 × 0
6. 6 × (10 – 6)
7. 6 × (12 – 3)
8. 6 × (13 – 8)

9. 6 × (16 – 8)
10. 6 × (13 – 6)
11. (6 × 4) + (7 × 6)
12. (6 × 5) + (6 × 8)

13. (4 × 6) + (6 × 2)
14. (9 × 6) + (3 × 6)
15. (6 × 9) + (8 × 6)
16. (6 × 5) + (9 × 6)

6.4

Multiplying by 9

A

1. 9 × 1	**5.** 9 × 6	**9.** 9 × 7	**13.** 5 × 9	**17.** 8 × 9
2. 9 × 2	**6.** 9 × 5	**10.** 9 × 8	**14.** 3 × 9	**18.** 2 × 9
3. 9 × 10	**7.** 9 × 3	**11.** 10 × 9	**15.** 6 × 9	**19.** 1 × 9
4. 9 × 4	**8.** 9 × 9	**12.** 4 × 9	**16.** 7 × 9	**20.** 0 × 9

B

Tables triangles look like this. Write the missing numbers, e.g.

1.
18
9 × ☐

3.

4 × 9
☐

5.
27
☐ × 9

27
3 × 9

2.
9 × 5
☐

4.
90
9 × ☐

6.
☐ × 9
36

7.
81
9 × ☐

8.
9 × ☐
72

C

Look at the number machine.
Copy and complete the tables.

→ In │ ×9 │Out→

1.

IN	5	10	6	9
OUT				

2.

IN				
OUT	63	54	72	81

3.

IN	3		5	
OUT		72		54

D

1. What is the fourth multiple of 9?
2. What is the seventh multiple of 9?
3. What is the ninth multiple of 9?
4. What is the tenth multiple of 9?
5. What is the twelfth multiple of 9?
6. What is the hundredth multiple of 9?
7. Which number is a multiple of 9 and 5?
8. Which number is a multiple of 7 and 9?

Multiplying by 3, 6 and 9

A

1. 3 × 5	**5.** 6 × 3	**9.** 6 × 2	**13.** 4 × 6	**17.** 9 × 2	**21.** 3 × 9
2. 3 × 3	**6.** 4 × 3	**10.** 6 × 5	**14.** 9 × 6	**18.** 9 × 5	**22.** 6 × 9
3. 3 × 8	**7.** 8 × 3	**11.** 6 × 3	**15.** 6 × 6	**19.** 9 × 10	**23.** 4 × 9
4. 3 × 7	**8.** 2 × 3	**12.** 6 × 7	**16.** 7 × 6	**20.** 9 × 3	**24.** 9 × 9

B

Write the answers.

1.	× 30	50	70	90	40	60
2.	× 60	20	30	50	60	90
3.	× 90	30	50	90	70	60

C

1. Which number less than 30 is a multiple of both 6 and 9?
2. Which numbers between 20 and 30 are multiples of both 3 and 6?
3. Which numbers between 10 and 30 are multiples of both 3 and 9?
4. Which numbers less than 50 are multiples of 9 and 6?
5. Which numbers between 50 and 100 are multiples of 3, 6 and 9?
6. Which number nearest to 100 is a multiple of 6 and 9?

D

Write the missing digit to make each number a multiple of 9.

1. 12☐	**4.** 32☐	**7.** 2☐7	**10.** 5☐6	**13.** ☐32
2. 17☐	**5.** 40☐	**8.** 4☐3	**11.** ☐64	**14.** ☐11
3. 23☐	**6.** 1☐3	**9.** 3☐1	**12.** ☐24	**15.** ☐05

E

1. What would half a dozen of A cost?
2. What would three each of B and C cost altogether?
3. What would nine of C and three of A cost altogether?
4. £42 was spent buying C. How many were bought?

A £8 B £7 C £6

Multiplying by 7

A

1. 7 × 1	**5.** 7 × 10	**9.** 7 × 8	**13.** 0 × 7	**17.** 1 × 7
2. 7 × 3	**6.** 7 × 4	**10.** 7 × 7	**14.** 3 × 7	**18.** 10 × 7
3. 7 × 2	**7.** 7 × 9	**11.** 2 × 7	**15.** 4 × 7	**19.** 8 × 7
4. 7 × 5	**8.** 7 × 6	**12.** 5 × 7	**16.** 6 × 7	**20.** 9 × 7

B

Copy and complete the tables. In  ×7 Out

1.

IN	5	8	7	9
OUT				

2.

IN				
OUT	35	21	70	56

3.

IN	6		3	
OUT		63		14

C

Multiply each number row by 7.

1. 2	7	0	6	4	10	3	5	8	9
2. 20	80	50	30	60	90	40	70	10	100

D

The arrow represents ×7. Write the missing numbers.

1. 4 ⟶ ⚫   **4.** 7 ⟶ ⚫   **7.** ⚫ ⟶ 49   **10.** ⚫ ⟶ 70

2. 2 ⟶ ⚫   **5.** 9 ⟶ ⚫   **8.** ⚫ ⟶ 63   **11.** ⚫ ⟶ 42

3. 8 ⟶ ⚫   **6.** ⚫ ⟶ 28   **9.** ⚫ ⟶ 35   **12.** ⚫ ⟶ 56

E

1. What is the third multiple of 7?

2. What is the sixth multiple of 7?

3. Which multiple of 7 is between 50 and 60?

4. Which multiple of 7 is between 60 and 70?

5. Which number is a multiple of both 6 and 7?

6. Which number is a multiple of both 9 and 7?

7. Which multiple of 7 is between 30 and 40?

6.7

Multiplying by 8

A

1. 8 × 10	**5.** 8 × 5	**9.** 8 × 6	**13.** 2 × 8	**17.** 8 × 8
2. 8 × 3	**6.** 8 × 7	**10.** 8 × 8	**14.** 10 × 8	**18.** 7 × 8
3. 8 × 2	**7.** 8 × 9	**11.** 1 × 8	**15.** 3 × 8	**19.** 9 × 8
4. 8 × 0	**8.** 8 × 4	**12.** 6 × 8	**16.** 5 × 8	**20.** 4 × 8

B

1. ×8	→	2	10	0	8	3	6	4	7	5	9
2. ×4 then double	→	1	3	5	2	9	4	8	6	7	10
3. Double, double then double again	→	0	2	10	4	3	5	9	7	8	6

C

Write two different multiplication facts for each number.

1. ☐ × ☐ ☐ × ☐   **4.** ☐ × ☐ ☐ × ☐

2. ☐ × ☐ ☐ × ☐   **5.** ☐ × ☐ ☐ × ☐

3. ☐ × ☐ 80 ☐ × ☐   **6.** ☐ × ☐ ☐ × ☐

D

Write the missing numbers.

1. 8 × ☐ = 0	**4.** 8 × ☐ = 16	**7.** 8 × ☐ = 24	**10.** 8 × ☐ = 32	**13.** ☐ × 8 = 24
2. 8 × ☐ = 80	**5.** ☐ × 8 = 0	**8.** ☐ × 8 = 16	**11.** 8 × ☐ = 40	**14.** ☐ × 8 = 64
3. ☐ × 8 = 48	**6.** ☐ × 8 = 8	**9.** ☐ × 8 = 72	**12.** 8 × ☐ = 56	**15.** 8 × ☐ = 48

E

True or false?

1. All multiples of 8 are even.

2. All multiples of 8 are also multiples of 4.

3. 60 is a multiple of both 10 and 8.

4. 100 is a multiple of 8.

5. Multiples of 8 are also multiples of 2.

6. 7 and 8 do not have a multiple which is the same.

6.8

Multiplying by All Tables

A

1. 2×9
2. 3×7
3. 5×5
4. 6×6

5. 4×5
6. 3×4
7. 2×6
8. 7×2

9. 4×5
10. 8×3
11. 7×1
12. 8×0

13. 10×10
14. 9×3
15. 6×8
16. 0×9

17. 5×7
18. 4×6
19. 3×10
20. 5×8

B

Write the answers to these more difficult tables.

1. 8×6
2. 7×9
3. 8×7
4. 4×9

5. 9×6
6. 8×8
7. 7×6
8. 8×4

9. 6×8
10. 9×4
11. 4×8
12. 7×8

13. 6×7
14. 6×9
15. 9×7
16. 7×7

17. 9×4
18. 9×8
19. 8×9
20. 4×9

C

Write the missing numbers.

1. $\square \times 2 = 14$
2. $\square \times 5 = 25$
3. $\square \times 10 = 60$

4. $\square \times 7 = 21$
5. $\square \times 6 = 36$
6. $5 \times \square = 40$

7. $3 \times \square = 9$
8. $7 \times \square = 28$
9. $9 \times \square = 81$

10. $8 \times \square = 32$
11. $\square \times 4 = 36$
12. $6 \times \square = 42$

13. $\square \times 9 = 45$
14. $8 \times \square = 64$
15. $\square \times 10 = 50$

D

1. $100 - (5 \times 7)$
2. $100 - (4 \times 8)$
3. $100 - (9 \times 9)$
4. $100 - (7 \times 8)$

5. $100 - (4 \times 3)$
6. $(7 \times 10) - 50$
7. $(10 \times 9) - 50$
8. $(9 \times 9) - 50$

9. $(7 \times 8) - 50$
10. $(8 \times 8) - 50$
11. $50 + (5 \times 5)$
12. $50 + (4 \times 9)$

13. $50 + (7 \times 7)$
14. $50 + (8 \times 6)$
15. $50 + (6 \times 9)$
16. $50 + (7 \times 8)$

E

Write the perimeter (p) and area (a) of each square.

1.
5 cm

p = ☐
a = ☐

2.
7 cm

p = ☐
a = ☐

3.
3 cm

p = ☐
a = ☐

4.
4 cm

p = ☐
a = ☐

5.
8 cm

p = ☐
a = ☐

6.9

Doubling and Halving

A ··

Double each number.

1. 12	**4.** 17	**7.** 18
2. 16	**5.** 10	**8.** 15
3. 11	**6.** 14	**9.** 13

Halve each number.

10. 30	**13.** 24	**16.** 28
11. 26	**14.** 32	**17.** 22
12. 38	**15.** 36	**18.** 40

B ··

1. Double ⟶ 38 42 33 46 28 31 47 34 25 49

2. Halve ⟶ 50 48 34 42 28 40 38 36 46 30

C ··

Write the numbers which leave the machines.

 → In | double | Out →

 → In | halve | Out →

IN	380	260	440	350	290	450
OUT						

IN	300	480	600	560	440	900
OUT						

D ··

Double each number.

1. 35	**3.** 65	**5.** 85	**7.** 25
2. 95	**4.** 45	**6.** 75	**8.** 75

Halve each number.

9. 70	**11.** 50	**13.** 110	**15.** 130
10. 190	**12.** 150	**14.** 90	**16.** 170

E ··

Write the missing numbers.

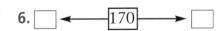
45 ◄— halve 90 double —► 180

1. ☐ ◄— 18 —► ☐   3. ☐ ◄— 36 —► ☐   5. ☐ ◄— 120 —► ☐

2. ☐ ◄— 40 —► ☐   4. ☐ ◄— 98 —► ☐   6. ☐ ◄— 170 —► ☐

Multiplying TU by 2, 3, 4 and 5

Key Skills ✔

Write the answers. Check them.

1. 4 × 2	**5.** 9 × 2	**9.** 8 × 3	**13.** 5 × 4	**17.** 7 × 5
2. 6 × 2	**6.** 3 × 3	**10.** 10 × 3	**14.** 9 × 4	**18.** 9 × 5
3. 8 × 2	**7.** 6 × 3	**11.** 6 × 4	**15.** 8 × 4	**19.** 6 × 5
4. 7 × 2	**8.** 9 × 3	**12.** 7 × 4	**16.** 8 × 5	**20.** 10 × 5

A ··········

Write the answers.

1. 20 × 2	**5.** 40 × 3	**9.** 80 × 5	**13.** 70 × 5	**17.** 80 × 4
2. 30 × 3	**6.** 50 × 4	**10.** 70 × 4	**14.** 60 × 4	**18.** 70 × 2
3. 30 × 2	**7.** 50 × 3	**11.** 60 × 3	**15.** 90 × 5	**19.** 60 × 5
4. 40 × 4	**8.** 50 × 2	**12.** 60 × 2	**16.** 30 × 5	**20.** 90 × 3

B ··········

1. (20 × 2) + (4 × 2)	**5.** (30 × 2) + (8 × 2)	**9.** (50 × 3) + (6 × 3)
2. (40 × 3) + (3 × 3)	**6.** (50 × 3) + (6 × 3)	**10.** (60 × 4) + (9 × 4)
3. (60 × 2) + (5 × 2)	**7.** (30 × 4) + (6 × 4)	**11.** (70 × 5) + (3 × 5)
4. (50 × 5) + (2 × 5)	**8.** (40 × 2) + (9 × 2)	**12.** (60 × 2) + (6 × 2)

C ··········

1. 42 × 2	**4.** 32 × 4	**7.** 35 × 2	**10.** 65 × 5	**13.** 85 × 4
2. 53 × 3	**5.** 81 × 5	**8.** 22 × 5	**11.** 92 × 5	**14.** 74 × 4
3. 61 × 2	**6.** 44 × 3	**9.** 47 × 4	**12.** 47 × 3	**15.** 59 × 2

D ··········

1. One game costs 45p.
What would three games cost?

2. One cup holds 65 m*l*.
What would five cups hold?

3. A quarter of a rod is 35 cm.
How long is the whole rod?

4. One ounce is about 25 g.
How many grams in five ounces?

5. Half price was £36.
What was the full price?

6. One child scored 47 points.
What would double the score be?

6.11

Multiplying TU by 6, 7, 8 and 9

Write the answers. Check them.

1. 2 × 6	**5.** 8 × 6	**9.** 8 × 7	**13.** 8 × 8	**17.** 5 × 9
2. 5 × 6	**6.** 7 × 7	**10.** 10 × 7	**14.** 4 × 8	**18.** 8 × 9
3. 4 × 6	**7.** 9 × 7	**11.** 3 × 8	**15.** 9 × 8	**19.** 7 × 9
4. 7 × 6	**8.** 6 × 7	**12.** 5 × 8	**16.** 6 × 9	**20.** 9 × 9

A

Write the answers.

1. 20 × 6	**5.** 80 × 6	**9.** 50 × 7	**13.** 50 × 8	**17.** 70 × 9
2. 60 × 6	**6.** 30 × 7	**10.** 80 × 7	**14.** 80 × 8	**18.** 80 × 9
3. 90 × 6	**7.** 40 × 7	**11.** 30 × 8	**15.** 70 × 8	**19.** 60 × 9
4. 50 × 6	**8.** 60 × 7	**12.** 90 × 8	**16.** 20 × 9	**20.** 90 × 9

B

1. (30 × 6) + (4 × 6)	**5.** (80 × 8) + (2 × 8)	**9.** (30 × 8) + (7 × 8)
2. (40 × 7) + (2 × 7)	**6.** (30 × 9) + (5 × 9)	**10.** (50 × 9) + (9 × 9)
3. (50 × 7) + (7 × 7)	**7.** (40 × 9) + (1 × 9)	**11.** (90 × 7) + (8 × 7)
4. (60 × 8) + (3 × 8)	**8.** (80 × 7) + (5 × 7)	**12.** (60 × 6) + (4 × 6)

C

1. 25 × 6	**5.** 49 × 7	**9.** 45 × 7	**13.** 37 × 8	**17.** 69 × 9
2. 35 × 6	**6.** 27 × 7	**10.** 71 × 7	**14.** 24 × 8	**18.** 73 × 9
3. 46 × 6	**7.** 36 × 7	**11.** 62 × 7	**15.** 47 × 8	**19.** 85 × 9
4. 57 × 6	**8.** 58 × 7	**12.** 49 × 7	**16.** 51 × 8	**20.** 63 × 9

D

1. 28 × 6	**5.** 56 × 8	**9.** 65 × 8	**13.** 72 × 7	**17.** 86 × 9
2. 37 × 9	**6.** 47 × 6	**10.** 78 × 9	**14.** 69 × 7	**18.** 35 × 6
3. 45 × 7	**7.** 37 × 7	**11.** 54 × 8	**15.** 54 × 8	**19.** 92 × 9
4. 25 × 6	**8.** 92 × 7	**12.** 66 × 9	**16.** 97 × 6	**20.** 86 × 8

Summary for Unit 6

Ⓐ ....

1. 7×2

2. 9×5

3. 7×10

4. 4×2

5. 8×5

6. 5×5

7. 9×2

8. 6×10

9. 9×10

10. 7×5

11. 8×10

12. 8×2

13. 5×2

14. 10×10

15. 6×5

16. 6×2

Ⓑ ....

Write the missing numbers.

1. $3 \times$ ⬭ $= 27$

2. $9 \times$ ⬭ $= 45$

3. $6 \times$ ⬭ $= 36$

4. $8 \times$ ⬭ $= 24$

5. ⬭ $\times 3 = 30$

6. ⬭ $\times 9 = 54$

7. ⬭ $\times 8 = 48$

8. ⬭ $\times 6 = 12$

9. ⬭ $\times 6 = 18$

10. ⬭ $\times 9 = 81$

11. $3 \times$ ⬭ $= 21$

12. $9 \times$ ⬭ $= 72$

Ⓒ ....

Copy and complete the tables.

1.

→ In | × 4 | Out →

IN	3		7	
OUT		24		36

2.

→ In | × 7 | Out →

IN	7		4	
OUT		7		49

3.

→ In | × 8 | Out →

IN	5		9	
OUT		64		32

Ⓓ ....

Double each number.

 18   46   97   35   260

Halve each number.

 38   90   76   150   900

Ⓔ ....

1. 47×2

2. 54×4

3. 65×5

4. 32×7

5. 58×3

6. 66×6

7. 35×9

8. 67×8

9. 83×8

10. 97×5

11. 47×9

12. 58×6

Knowledge needed
✓ multiplication facts
✓ multiplication and division are inverses

Helpful facts

Dividing by 2 (halving)
Dividing by 2 is the same as halving:

20 ÷ 2 = 10

half of 20 = 10

Halving odd numbers gives an answer with a half in it:

half of 5 = $2\frac{1}{2}$ half of 17 = $8\frac{1}{2}$

Remainders
These are the remainders possible when dividing by:

6	0, 1, 2, 3, 4, 5
7	0, 1, 2, 3, 4, 5, 6
8	0, 1, 2, 3, 4, 5, 6, 7
9	0, 1, 2, 3, 4, 5, 6, 7, 8
10	0, 1, 2, 3, 4, 5, 6, 7, 8, 9

Fractions
$\frac{1}{2}$ is the same as ÷ 2 $\frac{1}{2}$ of 8 = 4 $\frac{1}{3}$ is the same as ÷ 3 $\frac{1}{3}$ of 18 = 6

$\frac{1}{5}$ is the same as ÷ 5 $\frac{1}{5}$ of 25 = 5 $\frac{1}{4}$ is the same as ÷ 4 $\frac{1}{4}$ of 28 = 7

$\frac{1}{10}$ is the same as ÷ 10 $\frac{1}{10}$ of 90 = 9

Brackets

Work out the sum in the brackets first:

(36 ÷ 4) + 8 = 17

↑

work out first

9 + 8 = 17

Divisibility

All even numbers are exactly divisible by 2:
4, 12, 24, 36
All numbers which end in 5 or 0 are exactly divisible by 5:
5, 10, 20, 35, 60
All numbers which end in 0 are exactly divisible by 10:
10, 50, 80, 200

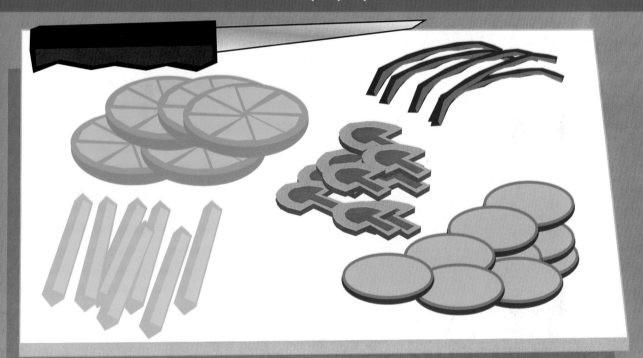

Learning outcomes for UNIT 7

✓ knows ÷2, ÷5, ÷10 within table facts by heart
✓ knows ÷3, ÷4, within table facts by heart
✓ knows ÷6, ÷7, ÷8, ÷9 within table facts, some by heart
✓ knows when to round up and round down remainders
✓ relates fractions of quantities to division facts
✓ knows multiplication and division are inverses
✓ halves odd numbers
✓ solves missing number problems
✓ rounds remainders sensibly
✓ solves division problems in context of money and measures
✓ knows some divisibility rules such as ÷2, ÷5, ÷10

Dividing by 2, 5 and 10

A

1. 10 ÷ 2
2. 10 ÷ 5
3. 60 ÷ 10
4. 14 ÷ 2

5. 15 ÷ 5
6. 40 ÷ 10
7. 12 ÷ 2
8. 16 ÷ 2

9. 25 ÷ 5
10. 50 ÷ 10
11. 35 ÷ 5
12. 30 ÷ 10

13. 18 ÷ 2
14. 80 ÷ 10
15. 40 ÷ 5
16. 30 ÷ 5

17. 70 ÷ 10
18. 45 ÷ 5
19. 90 ÷ 10
20. 20 ÷ 2

B

Copy and complete the missing numbers.

1. ☐ ÷ 2   △3   ☐ ÷ 5   ☐ ÷ 10

3. ☐ ÷ 2   △1   ☐ ÷ 5   ☐ ÷ 10

5. ☐ ÷ 2   △5   ☐ ÷ 5   ☐ ÷ 10

2. ☐ ÷ 2   △2   ☐ ÷ 5   ☐ ÷ 10

4. ☐ ÷ 2   △4   ☐ ÷ 5   ☐ ÷ 10

6. ☐ ÷ 2   △7   ☐ ÷ 5   ☐ ÷ 10

C

Work out the brackets first.

1. (6 ÷ 2) + (20 ÷ 5)
2. (50 ÷ 10) + (12 ÷ 2)
3. (90 ÷ 10) + (25 ÷ 5)
4. (8 ÷ 2) + (15 ÷ 5)

5. (40 ÷ 5) + (30 ÷ 10)
6. (45 ÷ 5) − (10 ÷ 5)
7. (20 ÷ 2) − (60 ÷ 10)
8. (80 ÷ 10) − (12 ÷ 2)

9. (70 ÷ 10) − (25 ÷ 5)
10. (60 ÷ 10) − (10 ÷ 2)
11. (80 ÷ 10) + (16 ÷ 2)
12. (45 ÷ 5) + (30 ÷ 10)

D

1. What is half 18?
2. What is 35 divided by 5?
3. How many tens in 60?
4. What is the remainder when 19 is divided by 2?

5. What is the remainder when 37 is divided by 10?
6. What is 30 divided by 5 then halved?

Dividing by 3 and 4

A

1. 6 ÷ 3
2. 3 ÷ 3
3. 9 ÷ 3
4. 15 ÷ 3

5. 21 ÷ 3
6. 12 ÷ 3
7. 27 ÷ 3
8. 24 ÷ 3

9. 18 ÷ 3
10. 30 ÷ 3
11. 4 ÷ 4
12. 8 ÷ 4

13. 16 ÷ 4
14. 12 ÷ 4
15. 20 ÷ 4
16. 24 ÷ 4

17. 32 ÷ 4
18. 28 ÷ 4
19. 40 ÷ 4
20. 36 ÷ 4

B

Write the missing numbers.

1. ▱ ÷ 4 = 4
2. ▱ ÷ 3 = 2
3. ▱ ÷ 4 = 3

4. ▱ ÷ 3 = 4
5. ▱ ÷ 3 = 6
6. ▱ ÷ 4 = 5

7. ▱ ÷ 3 = 7
8. ▱ ÷ 3 = 9
9. ▱ ÷ 4 = 8

10. ▱ ÷ 4 = 6
11. ▱ ÷ 3 = 3
12. ▱ ÷ 4 = 7

C

Divide by 3. Write the remainder.

1. 17   3. 16   5. 20   7. 26
2. 11   4. 18   6. 22   8. 29

Divide by 4. Write the remainder.

9. 19   11. 25   13. 30   15. 33
10. 17   12. 28   14. 34   16. 39

D

Work out the brackets first.

1. (24 ÷ 3) + (18 ÷ 3)
2. (16 ÷ 4) + (12 ÷ 4)
3. (36 ÷ 4) + (12 ÷ 3)

4. (15 ÷ 3) + (24 ÷ 4)
5. (20 ÷ 4) + (28 ÷ 4)
6. (21 ÷ 3) + (32 ÷ 4)

7. (36 ÷ 4) + (36 ÷ 4)
8. (21 ÷ 3) + (16 ÷ 4)
9. (27 ÷ 3) + (30 ÷ 3)

E

Copy and complete the tables.

1.

→ In | ÷4 | Out →

IN	28		36		40
OUT		6		3	

2.

→ In | ÷3 | Out →

IN	30		21		15
OUT		8		4	

Dividing by 6

A ....

Write how many sixes in each number.

1. 6	**3.** 12	**5.** 18	**7.** 48	**9.** 42
2. 24	**4.** 30	**6.** 36	**8.** 54	**10.** 60

B ....

Divide each number by 6. Write the remainder.

1. 19	**5.** 32	**9.** 37	**13.** 40	**17.** 53
2. 20	**6.** 36	**10.** 39	**14.** 43	**18.** 54
3. 26	**7.** 31	**11.** 46	**15.** 49	**19.** 57
4. 28	**8.** 33	**12.** 45	**16.** 50	**20.** 59

C ....

Divide each number by 3 then halve.

1. 6	**3.** 24	**5.** 30	**7.** 36	**9.** 48
2. 12	**4.** 18	**6.** 42	**8.** 54	**10.** 60

D ....

Look at the number machine.
Copy and complete the tables.

→ In | ÷6 |Out→

1.

IN	36	48	18	54
OUT				

2.

IN				
OUT	3	8	6	10

3.

IN		18		24
OUT	5		9	

E ....

Eggs are packed 6 to a box.
Write how many boxes are needed for these eggs.

1. 53	**3.** 28	**5.** 46	**7.** 63	**9.** 55
2. 47	**4.** 35	**6.** 57	**8.** 42	**10.** 50

7.4

Dividing by 9

A
1. 9 ÷ 9
2. 27 ÷ 9
3. 18 ÷ 9
4. 36 ÷ 9
5. 90 ÷ 9
6. 63 ÷ 9
7. 45 ÷ 9
8. 72 ÷ 9
9. 54 ÷ 9
10. 81 ÷ 9

B

Write how many nines are in each number.
1. 27
2. 9
3. 18
4. 45
5. 36
6. 63
7. 54
8. 81
9. 72
10. 90

C

Write the missing digit.

1. 2 ÷ 9 = 3r2

2. 4 ÷ 9 = 4r6

3. 2 ÷ 9 = 2r5

4. 3 ÷ 9 = 3r7

5. 5 ÷ 9 = 5r8

6. 4 ÷ 9 = 5r1

7. 3 ÷ 9 = 4r3

8. 7 ÷ 9 = 7r7

9. 6 ÷ 9 = 7r2

10. 8 ÷ 9 = 9r4

D

Use your number facts. Divide each number by 9.
1. 90
2. 450
3. 270
4. 360
5. 630
6. 540
7. 720
8. 180
9. 810
10. 900

E

Write true or false.
1. All odd numbers are exactly divisible by 9.
2. No even numbers are exactly divisible by 9.
3. 72 is divisible by both 9 and 8.
4. 35 is divisible by both 9 and 5.

7.5

Dividing by 7

A

Divide each number by 7.

1. 7	**3.** 35	**5.** 28	**7.** 56	**9.** 63
2. 14	**4.** 21	**6.** 42	**8.** 49	**10.** 70

B

Write the missing numbers.

1. ÷ 7 = 4 **3.** ÷ 7 = 3 **5.** ÷ 7 = 5 **7.** ÷ 7 = 6

2. ÷ 7 = 2 **4.** ÷ 7 = 7 **6.** ÷ 7 = 1 **8.** ÷ 7 = 8

C

Look at the number machine.
Copy and complete the tables.

→ In | ÷7 | Out →

1.

IN	35	56	21	49
OUT				

2.

IN				
OUT	8	2	9	4

3.

IN	70		28	
OUT		1		9

D

Write how many 7s in each number. Ignore the remainder.

1. 50	**4.** 25	**7.** 38	**10.** 48	**13.** 44
2. 20	**5.** 29	**8.** 22	**11.** 51	**14.** 69
3. 34	**6.** 61	**9.** 39	**12.** 57	**15.** 71

E

Divide each number by 7. Write the remainder.

1. 15	**4.** 25	**7.** 23	**10.** 61	**13.** 72
2. 18	**5.** 56	**8.** 32	**11.** 64	**14.** 53
3. 61	**6.** 40	**9.** 38	**12.** 44	**15.** 63

Dividing by 8

A

1. 8 ÷ 8
2. 24 ÷ 8
3. 80 ÷ 8
4. 16 ÷ 8
5. 40 ÷ 8
6. 32 ÷ 8
7. 56 ÷ 8
8. 48 ÷ 8
9. 72 ÷ 8
10. 64 ÷ 8

B

Write how many 8s are in each number.

1. 72
2. 24
3. 56
4. 40
5. 64
6. 48
7. 80
8. 32

C

Copy and complete the missing numbers. The arrow represents ÷ 8.

1. → 1
2. → 4
3. → 2
4. → 5
5. → 10
6. 24 →
7. 48 →
8. 72 →
9. 56 →
10. 64 →
11. → 9
12. → 6

D

Copy and complete the number chains. The arrow represents halve.

1. 24 → ☐ → ☐ → ☐
2. 32 → ☐ → ☐ → ☐
3. 40 → ☐ → ☐ → ☐
4. 16 → ☐ → ☐ → ☐
5. 72 → ☐ → ☐ → ☐
6. 48 → ☐ → ☐ → ☐
7. 64 → ☐ → ☐ → ☐
8. 80 → ☐ → ☐ → ☐

E

Divide each number by 8. Write the remainder.

1. 25
2. 28
3. 20
4. 32
5. 44
6. 34
7. 70
8. 75
9. 65
10. 43
11. 69
12. 61
13. 47
14. 27
15. 39
16. 37

7.7

Dividing Using All Tables

A

Write the answers.

1. $18 \div 2$ 4. $18 \div 9$ 7. $12 \div 2$ 10. $64 \div 8$ 13. $24 \div 3$

2. $50 \div 5$ 5. $49 \div 7$ 8. $42 \div 6$ 11. $81 \div 9$ 14. $35 \div 7$

3. $15 \div 3$ 6. $16 \div 4$ 9. $70 \div 10$ 12. $60 \div 10$ 15. $45 \div 5$

B

Write the missing numbers. The same number is needed twice.

1. $70 \div \square = \square \, r6$ 3. $83 \div \square = \square \, r2$ 5. $26 \div \square = \square \, r1$ 7. $38 \div \square = \square \, r2$

2. $52 \div \square = \square \, r3$ 4. $28 \div \square = \square \, r3$ 6. $19 \div \square = \square \, r3$ 8. $68 \div \square = \square \, r4$

C

Look at each number. Write two numbers which will divide exactly into it.

1. 32   4. 30   7. 42   10. 48   13. 54

2. 24   5. 35   8. 36   11. 56   14. 72

3. 15   6. 27   9. 45   12. 63   15. 90

D

Write the missing numbers.

1. $30 \div \bigcirc = 5$ 4. $40 \div \bigcirc = 10$ 7. $56 \div \bigcirc = 7$ 10. $50 \div \bigcirc = 5$

2. $81 \div \bigcirc = 9$ 5. $63 \div \bigcirc = 9$ 8. $48 \div \bigcirc = 6$ 11. $45 \div \bigcirc = 9$

3. $64 \div \bigcirc = 8$ 6. $32 \div \bigcirc = 4$ 9. $42 \div \bigcirc = 7$ 12. $72 \div \bigcirc = 8$

E

Copy and complete each table.

1.

÷	2	4
8		
12		
16		
24		

2.

÷	2	4
12		
18		
24		
36		

3.

÷	2	4
16		
24		
32		
48		

7.8

Remainders

A

1. 23 ÷ 3	**4.** 57 ÷ 8	**7.** 61 ÷ 10	**10.** 46 ÷ 6	**13.** 49 ÷ 5
2. 41 ÷ 5	**5.** 46 ÷ 9	**8.** 75 ÷ 9	**11.** 60 ÷ 9	**14.** 70 ÷ 9
3. 33 ÷ 6	**6.** 29 ÷ 7	**9.** 84 ÷ 8	**12.** 37 ÷ 4	**15.** 63 ÷ 8

B

Divide each number by 10. Write the remainder.

1. 73	**5.** 54	**9.** 103	**13.** 350	**17.** 717
2. 89	**6.** 134	**10.** 186	**14.** 468	**18.** 543
3. 64	**7.** 168	**11.** 235	**15.** 381	**19.** 616
4. 99	**8.** 195	**12.** 214	**16.** 632	**20.** 734

C

Write how much each person will receive.

Shared between 2. Shared amongst 3. Shared amongst 6.

1. 25p	**3.** 18p	**5.** 16p	**7.** 32p	**9.** 53p	**11.** 41p
2. 31p	**4.** 27p	**6.** 26p	**8.** 25p	**10.** 27p	**12.** 35p

D

Write how many boxes will be needed.

1. 15	**3.** 37	**5.** 30	**7.** 55	**9.** 47	**11.** 79
2. 26	**4.** 45	**6.** 46	**8.** 70	**10.** 63	**12.** 85

E

1. £7 is shared between Tom and Jo. How much will each get?
2. £3 is shared between four sisters. How much will each get?
3. Eggs are packed eight in a case. How many cases are needed for 28 eggs?
4. Five people can sit in a car. How many cars are needed for 22 people?

7.9

Number Problems

A ....

Each answer must be 20. Write the missing numbers.

1. (+ 17) ÷ 2   4. (– 6) ÷ 2   7. (÷ 3) + 13   10. (× 6) – 16

2. (÷ 3) + 16   5. (× 2) + 6   8. 5 × (– 13)   11. (– 18) × 2

3. (÷ 5) – 5   6. – (3 × 9)   9. (÷ 7) + 15   12. 50 – (× 10)

B ....

Find which pairs of numbers have:
1. A product of 63 and a total of 16.   5. A product of 48 and a total of 14.
2. A product of 40 and a total of 14.   6. A product of 36 and a total of 13.
3. A product of 21 and a total of 10.   7. A product of 24 and a total of 10.
4. A product of 56 and a total of 15.   8. A product of 72 and a total of 17.

C ....

1. How many 8p sweets can John buy for 70p?
2. Annisha buys 4 hankies costing 75p each.
   How much change does she get from £5?
3. Alex has 37 marbles. Sally has 20 more marbles than Alex.
   How many have they altogether?
4. Lee buys 4 books at £1.99 each and 3 books at £2.99 each.
   How much change from £20?

D ....

Only use odd digits and use + – × ÷ as often as you wish to make these answers.
1. 40   3. 36   5. 31   7. 24
2. 15   4. 78   6. 3   8. 16

Summary for Unit 7

A

Write the missing numbers.

1. ÷ 2 = 7   **4.** ÷ 2 = 10   **7.** 20 ÷ = 10   **10.** ÷ 2 = 3

2. ÷ 10 = 3   **5.** 5 ÷ = 1   **8.** 40 ÷ = 8   **11.** 60 ÷ = 6

3. ÷ 5 = 7   **6.** 80 ÷ = 8   **9.** 45 ÷ = 9   **12.** ÷ 5 = 9

B

Copy and complete each table.

→ In | ÷3 | Out →

1.

IN	30		21		27
OUT		2		8	

→ In | ÷4 | Out →

2.

IN	4		36		16
OUT		10		7	

C

1. Write how many sixes in 	60	30	48	36	24	54	18	42
2. Write how many sevens in →	49	70	42	28	21	56	35	63

D

Divide each number by 8.

1. 48   **3.** 40   **5.** 64   **7.** 24

2. 72   **4.** 56   **6.** 32   **8.** 80

Divide each number by 9.

9. 90   **11.** 63   **13.** 72   **15.** 27

10. 45   **12.** 36   **14.** 54   **16.** 81

E

Write the remainder.

1. 17 ÷ 2   **4.** 39 ÷ 6   **7.** 25 ÷ 7   **10.** 30 ÷ 8   **13.** 41 ÷ 7

2. 21 ÷ 4   **5.** 48 ÷ 5   **8.** 37 ÷ 5   **11.** 45 ÷ 8   **14.** 70 ÷ 9

3. 64 ÷ 10   **6.** 22 ÷ 3   **9.** 45 ÷ 6   **12.** 34 ÷ 4   **15.** 29 ÷ 3

Fractions

Helpful facts

>< = symbols

> means is larger than

< means is smaller than

= means is equal to

$$\frac{1}{3} > \frac{1}{4} \qquad \frac{1}{2} < \frac{3}{4} \qquad \frac{1}{2} = \frac{4}{8}$$

Equivalent fractions

Some fractions are worth the same even though they may look different:

$$\frac{1}{2} = \frac{2}{4} = \frac{3}{6} = \frac{4}{8}$$

$$\frac{1}{3} = \frac{2}{6} = \frac{3}{9} = \frac{4}{12}$$

$$\frac{1}{4} = \frac{2}{8} = \frac{3}{12} = \frac{4}{16}$$

$$\frac{1}{5} = \frac{2}{10} = \frac{3}{15} = \frac{4}{20}$$

Equivalent strips

Equivalent strips help to compare fractions which are the same:

half
quarter
eighth

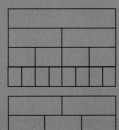

half
third
sixth

half
fifth
tenth

Fractions of quantities

$\frac{1}{2}$ is the same as $\div 2$

$\frac{1}{4}$ is the same as $\div 4$

$\frac{1}{3}$ is the same as $\div 3$

Mixed numbers

These are whole numbers and fractions: $1\frac{3}{4}, 2\frac{1}{3}, 4\frac{7}{8}$

Mixed numbers can be changed to top heavy (or improper) fractions:

$$1\frac{2}{3} = \frac{5}{3} \qquad 2\frac{3}{4} = \frac{11}{4}$$

Rounding

If the fraction is less than $\frac{1}{2}$, round down.
If the fraction is $\frac{1}{2}$ or more, round up:

$4\frac{1}{8}$ metres ≈ 4 metres

$1\frac{3}{4}$ kg ≈ 2 kg

Remainders

Remainders can be written as a fraction:

$$13 \div 4 = \frac{13}{4} = 3\frac{1}{4}$$

$$11 \div 3 = \frac{11}{3} = 3\frac{2}{3}$$

Learning outcomes for UNIT 8

✓ recognises simple fractions e.g. $\frac{1}{2}$, $\frac{1}{3}$, $\frac{1}{4}$

✓ recognises fractions of shapes

✓ finds simple fractions of quantities

✓ knows equivalence of simple fractions $\frac{3}{4} = \frac{6}{8}$

✓ compares and orders fractions $\frac{1}{2} > \frac{1}{3}$ $\frac{1}{4} < \frac{1}{3}$

✓ knows mixed numbers $1\frac{3}{4} = \frac{7}{4}$

✓ writes a remainder as a fraction

Fractions of Shapes

A ....

Write the fraction which has been shaded.

1.

3.

5.

7.

2.

4.

6.

8.

B ....

Write the fraction which has been shaded.

1.

3.

5.

2.

4.

6.

C ....

Find matching pairs of strips which show the same fraction.
Write which pairs go together.

A

B

C

D

E

F

Fractions of Shapes

Write which pairs go together.

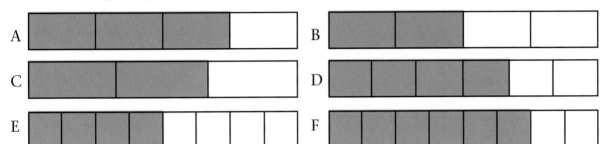

A

B

C

D

E

F

E

Match each shape to one of the seven fractions.

$\frac{1}{8}$ $\frac{1}{4}$ $\frac{3}{8}$ $\frac{1}{2}$ $\frac{5}{8}$ $\frac{3}{4}$ $\frac{7}{8}$

1.

3.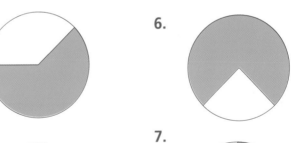

6.

2.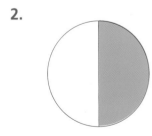

4.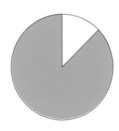

7.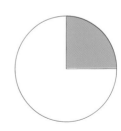

5.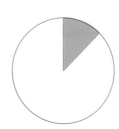

89

Fractions of Quantities

A

Write the answers.

$\frac{1}{2}$ of

| **1.** 26 | **3.** 46 | **5.** 88 | **7.** 68 | **9.** 90 |
| **2.** 34 | **4.** 54 | **6.** 48 | **8.** 70 | **10.** 36 |

$\frac{1}{4}$ of

| **11.** 28 | **13.** 36 | **15.** 24 | **17.** 16 | **19.** 100 |
| **12.** 60 | **14.** 80 | **16.** 32 | **18.** 20 | **20.** 40 |

B

Write the answers.

$\frac{1}{3}$ of:		$\frac{1}{8}$ of:		$\frac{1}{10}$ of:	
1. £12	**3.** £30	**5.** 24 cm	**7.** 80 cm	**9.** 50 m	**11.** 120 m
2. £21	**4.** £24	**6.** 32 cm	**8.** 56 cm	**10.** 80 m	**12.** 250 m

C

Write remainders as fractions, e.g. $11 \div 4 = 2\frac{3}{4}$

1. $9 \div 2$	**5.** $31 \div 2$	**9.** $31 \div 3$	**13.** $23 \div 5$	**17.** $19 \div 4$
2. $15 \div 2$	**6.** $16 \div 3$	**10.** $19 \div 3$	**14.** $34 \div 5$	**18.** $21 \div 4$
3. $23 \div 2$	**7.** $22 \div 3$	**11.** $14 \div 5$	**15.** $41 \div 5$	**19.** $10 \div 4$
4. $27 \div 2$	**8.** $25 \div 3$	**12.** $18 \div 5$	**16.** $13 \div 4$	**20.** $18 \div 4$

D

| **1.** $\frac{1}{2}$ of £7 | **3.** $\frac{1}{10}$ of 50 cm | **5.** $\frac{1}{2}$ of 25 cm | **7.** $\frac{1}{2}$ of 60 mins |
| **2.** $\frac{1}{3}$ of £15 | **4.** $\frac{1}{4}$ of 30 cm | **6.** $\frac{1}{3}$ of 60 mins | **8.** $\frac{1}{10}$ of 60 mins |

E

| **1.** $\frac{1}{2}$ of 32 | **2.** $\frac{1}{2}$ of 40 | **3.** $\frac{1}{2}$ of 56 | **4.** $\frac{1}{2}$ of 60 |
| $\frac{1}{4}$ of 32 | $\frac{1}{8}$ of 40 | $\frac{1}{4}$ of 56 | $\frac{1}{3}$ of 60 |

8.3

Mixed Numbers

A ....

Write these shaded parts as mixed fractions.

1.   ⬤⬤◑

4.   ⬤⬤◕

7.   ⬤⬤⬤◔

2.   ⬤◔

5.   ⬤⬤⬤◑

8.   ⬤⬤⬤⬤◔

3.   ⬤⬤⬤◔

6.   ⬤⬤◔

B ....

Change these whole numbers into fractions.

Halves.		Quarters.		Thirds.		Tenths.	
1. 1	3. 5	5. 1	7. 4	9. 1	11. 9	13. 1	15. 3
2. 3	4. 10	6. 2	8. 8	10. 3	12. 10	14. 4	16. 9

C ....

Write how many halves.   Write how many thirds.   Write how many quarters.

1. $2\frac{1}{2}$ 3. $9\frac{1}{2}$ 5. $1\frac{2}{3}$ 7. $3\frac{1}{3}$ 9. $1\frac{1}{4}$ 11. $5\frac{3}{4}$

2. $3\frac{1}{2}$ 4. 10   6. $4\frac{1}{3}$ 8. 7   10. $3\frac{3}{4}$ 12. 6

D ....

Change to mixed numbers.

1. $\frac{5}{2}$ 4. $\frac{17}{2}$ 7. $\frac{18}{5}$ 10. $\frac{19}{8}$ 13. $\frac{23}{10}$

2. $\frac{9}{2}$ 5. $\frac{7}{5}$ 8. $\frac{28}{5}$ 11. $\frac{35}{8}$ 14. $\frac{39}{10}$

3. $\frac{15}{2}$ 6. $\frac{14}{5}$ 9. $\frac{13}{8}$ 12. $\frac{17}{10}$ 15. $\frac{41}{10}$

Equivalences of Fractions

A ....

Write the pairs of fractions as equivalences.

1.

4.

7.

2.

5.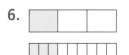

8.

3.

6.

9.

B ....

Copy and complete the fraction chains.

1. $\dfrac{1}{2} = \dfrac{\square}{4} = \dfrac{\square}{6} = \dfrac{\square}{8}$

3. $\dfrac{1}{4} = \dfrac{\square}{8} = \dfrac{\square}{12} = \dfrac{\square}{16}$

5. $\dfrac{1}{8} = \dfrac{\square}{16} = \dfrac{\square}{24} = \dfrac{\square}{32}$

2. $\dfrac{1}{3} = \dfrac{\square}{6} = \dfrac{\square}{9} = \dfrac{\square}{12}$

4. $\dfrac{1}{5} = \dfrac{\square}{10} = \dfrac{\square}{15} = \dfrac{\square}{20}$

6. $\dfrac{1}{10} = \dfrac{\square}{20} = \dfrac{\square}{30} = \dfrac{\square}{40}$

C ....

Write the missing numbers.

1. $\dfrac{3}{4} = \dfrac{\square}{8}$

3. $\dfrac{3}{8} = \dfrac{\square}{16}$

5. $\dfrac{7}{10} = \dfrac{\square}{100}$

7. $\dfrac{2}{5} = \dfrac{\square}{30}$

2. $\dfrac{2}{3} = \dfrac{\square}{9}$

4. $\dfrac{2}{5} = \dfrac{\square}{10}$

6. $\dfrac{3}{4} = \dfrac{\square}{12}$

8. $\dfrac{5}{8} = \dfrac{\square}{16}$

D ....

Write true or false: = equals   < is smaller than   > is bigger than

1. $\dfrac{1}{2} = \dfrac{5}{8}$

3. $\dfrac{3}{4} = \dfrac{6}{8}$

5. $\dfrac{3}{4} < \dfrac{1}{3}$

7. $\dfrac{1}{3} < \dfrac{1}{8}$

9. $\dfrac{2}{3} > \dfrac{1}{4}$

2. $\dfrac{1}{2} > \dfrac{4}{8}$

4. $\dfrac{3}{4} > \dfrac{1}{2}$

6. $\dfrac{1}{3} = \dfrac{4}{12}$

8. $\dfrac{2}{3} = \dfrac{3}{5}$

10. $\dfrac{2}{3} < \dfrac{1}{2}$

Fractions and Measures

A

1. $1\frac{1}{2}$ metres = ☐ cm

2. $\frac{3}{4}$ metre = ☐ cm

3. $\frac{1}{5}$ metre = ☐ cm

4. $\frac{7}{10}$ metre = ☐ cm

5. $1\frac{1}{4}$ litres = ☐ ml

6. $2\frac{3}{4}$ litres = ☐ ml

7. $1\frac{1}{2}$ litres = ☐ ml

8. $\frac{1}{10}$ litre = ☐ ml

9. $1\frac{1}{2}$ kg = ☐ g

10. $\frac{3}{4}$ kg = ☐ g

11. $\frac{1}{4}$ kg = ☐ g

12. $\frac{1}{5}$ kg = ☐ g

B

1. $\frac{1}{2}$ hour = mins

2. $\frac{3}{4}$ hour = mins

3. $\frac{1}{4}$ hour = mins

4. $\frac{1}{3}$ hour = mins

5. $\frac{1}{2}$ min = secs

6. $\frac{1}{4}$ min = secs

7. $\frac{3}{4}$ min = secs

8. $\frac{1}{10}$ min = secs

9. $\frac{1}{2}$ day = hours

10. $\frac{1}{4}$ day = hours

11. $\frac{3}{4}$ day = hours

12. $\frac{1}{3}$ day = hours

C

Write each fraction to the nearest whole unit.

1. $4\frac{3}{4}$ kg

2. $2\frac{1}{3}$ kg

3. $5\frac{5}{8}$ kg

4. $3\frac{3}{8}$ kg

5. $1\frac{3}{10}$ metres

6. $3\frac{7}{10}$ metres

7. $4\frac{1}{10}$ metres

8. $6\frac{9}{10}$ metres

9. $2\frac{1}{3}$ litres

10. $3\frac{1}{2}$ litres

11. $4\frac{7}{8}$ litres

12. $1\frac{1}{5}$ litres

13. $1\frac{2}{3}$ hr

14. $2\frac{1}{4}$ hr

15. $4\frac{1}{2}$ hr

16. $3\frac{3}{4}$ hr

Fractions and Measures

D ....

Each pole is half as long as the one before.
Write the length of the shortest pole.

1.

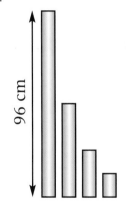

64 cm

3.

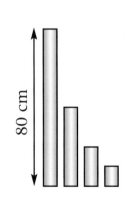

88 cm

5.

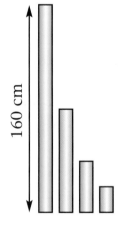

120 cm

2.

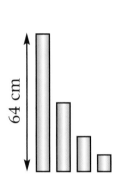

96 cm

4.

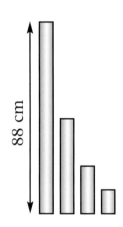

80 cm

6.

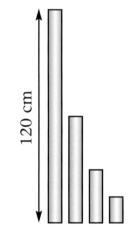

160 cm

Summary for Unit 8

A

Write the fraction which has been shaded.

1.

2.

3.

4.

B

1. One half of 36.

2. One quarter of 24.

3. One third of 90.

4. One eighth of £16.

5. One tenth of £60.

6. One fifth of £45.

C

Change to mixed numbers ⟶ 1. $\frac{17}{2}$ 2. $\frac{19}{3}$ 3. $\frac{15}{8}$ 4. $\frac{38}{10}$

Change to improper fractions ⟶ 5. $2\frac{1}{2}$ 6. $3\frac{3}{4}$ 7. $1\frac{3}{8}$ 8. $2\frac{3}{10}$

D

Write the missing numbers.

1. $\frac{1}{2} = \frac{\square}{6}$

2. $\frac{3}{8} = \frac{\square}{16}$

3. $\frac{3}{10} = \frac{\square}{100}$

4. $\frac{3}{4} = \frac{\square}{8}$

E

1. $\frac{3}{4}$ of 1 metre = ▨ cm

2. $\frac{2}{3}$ of 1 hour = ▨ mins

3. $\frac{3}{10}$ of 1 litre = ▨ ml

4. $\frac{1}{2}$ of 1 kilogram = ▨ g

5. $\frac{3}{5}$ of 1 min = ▨ secs

6. $\frac{1}{2}$ of 1 cm = ▨ mm

Simple Decimals

Knowledge needed
✓ place value

Helpful facts

Decimal point

The decimal point separates

- whole numbers
  from parts of numbers:

whole   part of
number   number

5 . 1

- pounds from pennies:

pound   pence

£6 . 72

Halves

A half is the same as
five tenths:

$$\frac{1}{2} = \frac{5}{10} = 0.5$$

Tenths

The decimal point
comes between whole
numbers and tenths:

whole ↘   ↗ tenth
number   8 . 4

Hundredths

Hundredths is that place to
the right of the tenth units:

units . tenths hundredths

$$0 . 4 \, 2 = \frac{42}{100}$$

↗   ↖
4 tenths   2 hundredths

Writing fractions as decimals

Tenths and hundredths can be
written as decimals:

$$\frac{3}{10} = 0.3$$

$$\frac{55}{100} = 0.55$$

$$\frac{7}{100} = 0.07$$

Writing decimals as fractions

Decimals can be
written as fractions:

$$0.7 = \frac{7}{10} \qquad 0.5 = \frac{5}{10} = \frac{1}{2}$$

$$0.71 = \frac{71}{100} \qquad 0.25 = \frac{25}{100} = \frac{1}{4}$$

Common fractions and decimals

$$\frac{1}{2} = 0.50 \qquad \frac{1}{4} = 0.25$$

$$\frac{1}{10} = 0.1 \qquad \frac{3}{4} = 0.75$$

$\frac{1}{3}$ makes a special
sort of decimal number
0.333333…

The numbers
go on and on – it is recurring.

Remainders

Remainders can be written as decimals:

$13 \div 5 = \dfrac{13}{5} = 2.6$

Rounding to the nearest whole

If the decimal is less than $\dfrac{1}{2}$ or 0.5, round down

otherwise round up:

$3.28 \approx 3.0$

$4.7 \approx 5.0$

$8.5 \approx 9.0$

Learning outcomes for UNIT 9

✓ knows tenths as fractions and decimals

✓ knows hundredths as fractions and decimals

✓ recognises simple fractions as decimals, e.g. $\dfrac{1}{2}, \dfrac{1}{4}, \dfrac{3}{4}$

✓ recognises decimals in context of money and measures

✓ rounds decimals to nearest whole number

✓ knows equivalence in measures which use decimals

9.1

Decimals and Tenths

A

Write how many tenths these displays show.

1. 0.1
2. 0.5
3. 0.7

4. 0.4
5. 0.2
6. 0.6

7. 0.3
8. 0.8
9. 0.9

B

Write these as decimals.

1. $\frac{2}{10}$
2. $\frac{5}{10}$

3. $\frac{1}{10}$
4. $\frac{3}{10}$

5. $\frac{4}{10}$
6. $\frac{7}{10}$

7. $\frac{8}{10}$
8. $\frac{9}{10}$

9. $\frac{6}{10}$
10. $\frac{10}{10}$

C

Write these as decimals.

1. $1\frac{5}{10}$
2. $1\frac{7}{10}$
3. $2\frac{3}{10}$
4. $4\frac{1}{10}$

5. $5\frac{2}{10}$
6. $2\frac{8}{10}$
7. $1\frac{6}{10}$
8. $3\frac{5}{10}$

9. $2\frac{4}{10}$
10. $3\frac{6}{10}$
11. $5\frac{7}{10}$
12. $2\frac{7}{10}$

13. $6\frac{8}{10}$
14. $1\frac{9}{10}$
15. $4\frac{3}{10}$
16. $1\frac{2}{10}$

17. $4\frac{4}{10}$
18. $3\frac{9}{10}$
19. $7\frac{3}{10}$
20. $2\frac{1}{10}$

D

Write to which decimal numbers the arrows point.

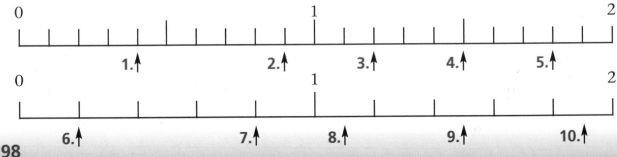

98

Decimals and Hundredths

A

Write how many hundredths these displays show.

1. 0.25
2. 0.75
3. 0.65
4. 0.84
5. 0.13
6. 0.60
7. 0.44
8. 0.05
9. 0.97

B

Write these as decimals.

1. $\frac{35}{100}$
2. $\frac{75}{100}$
3. $\frac{20}{100}$
4. $\frac{73}{100}$
5. $\frac{67}{100}$
6. $\frac{91}{100}$
7. $\frac{3}{100}$
8. $\frac{8}{100}$

C

Write how many pennies are in these amounts.

1. £0.50
2. £0.45
3. £0.35
4. £0.85
5. £0.46
6. £0.72
7. £0.91
8. £0.06
9. £1.45
10. £2.50
11. £3.75
12. £2.80
13. £3.70
14. £2.35
15. £1.76

D

Write these pennies as pounds.

1. 30p
2. 70p
3. 60p
4. 40p
5. 25p
6. 65p
7. 75p
8. 136p
9. 208p
10. 310p
11. 426p
12. 236p
13. 177p
14. 204p
15. 130p

E

Write to which decimal number the arrows point.

0   1

1.↑   2.↑   3.↑   4.↑   5.↑

9.3

Decimals and Measures

A

Write the length of each rod in centimetres.

1.

2.

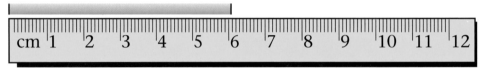

3.

B

Write these fractions as decimals.

1. $1\frac{1}{2}$ m = ☐ m

2. $2\frac{1}{4}$ m = ☐ m

3. $1\frac{3}{4}$ m = ☐ m

4. $2\frac{1}{10}$ m = ☐ m

5. $\frac{3}{4}$ kg = ☐ kg

6. $\frac{1}{2}$ kg = ☐ kg

7. $\frac{1}{4}$ kg = ☐ kg

8. $\frac{3}{10}$ kg = ☐ kg

9. $2\frac{1}{2}$ cm = ☐ cm

10. $4\frac{1}{4}$ cm = ☐ cm

11. $1\frac{3}{4}$ cm = ☐ cm

12. $2\frac{9}{10}$ cm = ☐ cm

C

Round each amount to the nearest whole number.

1. £7.56
2. £4.38
3. £6.74
4. £8.09

5. 3.65 m
6. 8.50 m
7. 6.49 m
8. 5.80 m

9. 1.5 kg
10. 6.35 kg
11. 4.25 kg
12. 3.75 kg

13. 6.3 km
14. 8.05 km
15. 6.5 km
16. 3.72 km

9.4

Decimal Notation and Measuring

A

Write how much is in each container.

1.

2.

3.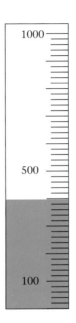

4.

B

Read the weight shown on each dial.

1.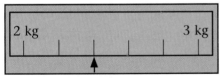

2.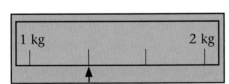

3.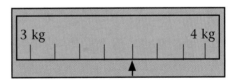

4.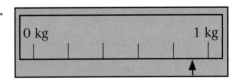

C

Write the missing numbers.

1. 0.5 m = ☐ cm

2. 0.25 m = ☐ cm

3. 0.36 m = ☐ cm

4. 0.04 m = ☐ cm

5. £0.50 = ☐ p

6. £1.25 = ☐ p

7. £2.04 = ☐ p

8. £0.06 = ☐ p

9. 2.5 cm = ☐ mm

10. 1.6 cm = ☐ mm

11. 3.0 cm = ☐ mm

12. 0.4 cm = ☐ mm

Decimal Problems

A ....

Write as decimals.   Write as fractions.

1. $\frac{1}{2}$ **3.** $\frac{1}{10}$ **5.** $1\frac{3}{4}$ **7.** 0.25   **9.** 0.50   **11.** 3.25

2. $\frac{1}{4}$ **4.** $2\frac{1}{4}$ **6.** $4\frac{1}{2}$ **8.** 0.75   **10.** 1.5   **12.** 6.10

B ....

Write these in order.
Start with the smallest.

1. 0.4   4.0   0.04   **5.** 2.6   0.6   0.2

2. 2.3   3.2   0.23   **6.** 4.5   5.0   4.0

3. 0.45   5.4   0.5   **7.** 3.6   6.3   0.6

4. 3.1   1.3   0.31   **8.** 0.07   0.7   0.30

C ....

Divide and write remainders as decimals.

1. 11 ÷ 2   **6.** 7 ÷ 4   **11.** 6 ÷ 5   **16.** 13 ÷ 10

2. 23 ÷ 2   **7.** 9 ÷ 4   **12.** 9 ÷ 5   **17.** 47 ÷ 10

3. 17 ÷ 2   **8.** 15 ÷ 4   **13.** 13 ÷ 5   **18.** 26 ÷ 10

4. 9 ÷ 2   **9.** 21 ÷ 4   **14.** 22 ÷ 5   **19.** 35 ÷ 10

5. 15 ÷ 2   **10.** 22 ÷ 4   **15.** 16 ÷ 5   **20.** 68 ÷ 10

D ....

1. A rail is 2 metres long. A piece measuring 0.5 metres is cut off.
How much remains?

2. A piece of wool 4.5 metres long is cut into two equal pieces.
How long is each piece?

3. £1.80 is shared equally between two people. How much does each get?

4. Stuart weighs 38.5 kg and Lucy weighs 38.25 kg. Who is the heavier?

Summary for Unit 9

A

Write how many tenths.

1. 0.6 **2.** 0.7 **3.** 0.4 **4.** 0.3

Write as decimals.

5. $\frac{3}{10}$ **6.** $\frac{7}{10}$ **7.** $\frac{9}{10}$ **8.** $\frac{1}{10}$

B

Write as decimals.

1 $\frac{45}{100}$ **3.** $3\frac{25}{100}$

2. $2\frac{50}{100}$ **4.** $2\frac{46}{100}$

Write these pennies as pounds.

5. 136p **7.** 350p

6. 427p **8.** 25p

C

Write as decimals.

1. $2\frac{1}{2}$ metres

2. $4\frac{1}{2}$ metres

3. $1\frac{1}{4}$ metres

Write as decimals.

4. $1\frac{1}{2}$ kg

5. $2\frac{1}{4}$ kg

6. $1\frac{3}{4}$ kg

Round each amount to the nearest pound.

7. £3.62

8. £4.09

9. £8.50

D

Write the measurements.

1.

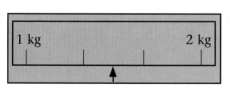

1 kg   2 kg

2.

1000

500

100

E

Write as decimals.

1. 19 ÷ 2 **3.** 17 ÷ 5
2. 13 ÷ 4 **4.** 73 ÷ 10

Write as decimals.

5. $\frac{3}{10}$ **7.** $\frac{6}{10}$

6. $\frac{3}{4}$ **8.** $\frac{1}{4}$

Write as fractions.

9. 0.5 **11.** 0.3

10. 0.25 **12.** 0.75

Answers

page 18 . . . .

1. 4 tens	**3.** 7 hundreds	**5.** 302	**7.** 96
2. 4 units	**4.** 9 tens	**6.** 650	**8.** 715

page 19 . . . .

1. 2104	**3.** 3620	**5.** 3 thousands
2. 4033	**4.** 7 hundreds	**6.** 2 tens

page 30 . . . .

1. 11	**4.** 17	**7.** 18	**10.** 18	**13.** 17
2. 16	**5.** 11	**8.** 15	**11.** 19	**14.** 17
3. 12	**6.** 16	**9.** 17	**12.** 20	**15.** 19

page 31 . . . .

1. 6	**5.** 10	**9.** 8	**13.** 12	**17.** 10
2. 8	**6.** 7	**10.** 9	**14.** 18	**18.** 13
3. 9	**7.** 9	**11.** 10	**15.** 15	**19.** 13
4. 8	**8.** 8	**12.** 14	**16.** 11	**20.** 17

page 34 . . . .

1. 11	**5.** 12	**9.** 10	**13.** 5	**17.** 5
2. 12	**6.** 14	**10.** 9	**14.** 8	**18.** 3
3. 17	**7.** 7	**11.** 8	**15.** 6	**19.** 5
4. 11	**8.** 10	**12.** 10	**16.** 5	**20.** 19

Answers

page 35 . . . .

1. 12	**4.** 11	**7.** 5	**10.** 9	**13.** 11
2. 13	**5.** 12	**8.** 9	**11.** 9	**14.** 12
3. 11	**6.** 8	**9.** 9	**12.** 6	**15.** 15

page 42 . . . .

1. 16	**3.** 11	**5.** 15	**7.** 110	**9.** 80
2. 11	**4.** 10	**6.** 70	**8.** 160	**10.** 140

page 43 . . . .

1. 71	**3.** 64	**5.** 71	**7.** 71	**9.** 107
2. 65	**4.** 64	**6.** 74	**8.** 88	**10.** 123

page 45 . . . .

1. 15	**3.** 10	**5.** 13	**7.** 140	**9.** 110
2. 18	**4.** 11	**6.** 90	**8.** 170	**10.** 160

page 53 . . . .

1. 5	**4.** 1	**7.** 40	**10.** 20	**13.** 79
2. 5	**5.** 0	**8.** 50	**11.** 14	**14.** 66
3. 7	**6.** 30	**9.** 20	**12.** 26	**15.** 43

Answers

. . . .

1. 5	**3.** 8	**5.** 7	**7.** 20	**9.** 60
2. 8	**4.** 2	**6.** 20	**8.** 20	**10.** 10

. . . .

1. 8	**3.** 4	**5.** 4	**7.** 30	**9.** 20
2. 6	**4.** 4	**6.** 20	**8.** 40	**10.** 80

. . . .

1. 8	**5.** 18	**9.** 24	**13.** 20	**17.** 35
2. 12	**6.** 9	**10.** 30	**14.** 36	**18.** 45
3. 16	**7.** 18	**11.** 24	**15.** 32	**19.** 30
4. 14	**8.** 27	**12.** 28	**16.** 40	**20.** 50

. . . .

1. 12	**5.** 48	**9.** 56	**13.** 64	**17.** 45
2. 30	**6.** 49	**10.** 70	**14.** 32	**18.** 72
3. 24	**7.** 63	**11.** 24	**15.** 72	**19.** 63
4. 42	**8.** 42	**12.** 40	**16.** 54	**20.** 81

Detailed Topic Guide

Detailed Topic Guide

Detailed Topic Guide